taming & training budgerigars

cessa feyeraband
and
dr. matthew m. vriends

Pictorial Credits:

Black and White: Dr. F. Goethe: 121; Herald-Sun: 188; Harry V. Lacey: 9, 27, 55, 66, 124, 139, 140, 147, 151, 153, 154, 157, 159, 164, 165, 168, 172, 181 (below), 184; Three Lions: 1; Louise van der Meid: 7, 23, 34, 43, 70, 71, 95, 98, 100, 122, 128, 130, 132, 143, 144, 146, 148, 158, 180, 181 (above), 190, 191; Horst Mueller: 12, 74, 75, 78, 79, 82, 83, 86 (above), 91, 155; Berta Ragotzi: 86 (below); John Rammel: 15, 137, 160; George L. Wetzel: 24, 25.

Color: Dr. G. Allen: 33 (above), 92; Dr. Herbert R. Axelrod: 166, 167; Hanson: 93; Harry V. Lacey: 41, 45, 182, 186; Louise van der Meid: 60, 187; Horst Mueller: 33 (below), 36, 37, 40, 44, 48, 49, 52, 53, 56, 57, 61, 64, 65, 69, 76, 77, 88, 89, 170, 174, 175, 178, 179; San Diego Zoo: 162, 163; Ralph Small: 96; R.A. Vowles: 84, 171; From Bird Diseases, by L. Arnall and I.F. Keymer: 72, 73.

Line illustrations by E. Bohlman Patterson.

Cover photo by Tierfreunde.

Based on *The Budgerigar as a Pet,* by Cessa Feyerabend.

ISBN 0-87666-960-7

Distributed in the U.S.A. by T.F.H. Publications, Inc., 211 West Sylvania Avenue, P.O. Box 27, Neptune City, N.J. 07753; in England by T.F.H. (Gt. Britain) Ltd., 13 Nutley Lane, Reigate, Surrey; in Canada to the book store and library trade by Clarke, Irwin & Company, Clarwin House, 791 St. Clair Avenue West, Toronto 10, Ontario; in Canada to the pet trade by Rolf C. Hagen Ltd., 3225 Sartelon Street, Montreal 382, Quebec; in Southeast Asia by Y.W. Ong, 9 Lorong 36 Geylang, Singapore 14; in Australia and the south Pacific by Pet Imports Pty. Ltd., P.O. Box 149, Brookvale 2100, N.S.W., Australia. Published by T.F.H. Publications, Inc. Ltd., The British Crown Colony of Hong Kong

Contents

I The Budgerigar as a Talker

The budgerigar is the pretty little bird generally called lovebird or parrakeet which is found in practically every bird store and kept in many homes. He should not be called lovebird since the real lovebird is the African, which is heavier and has a short tail. If he is to be called parrakeet, he should be called Australian Shell Parrakeet since there are many different kinds of parrakeets. The best name is budgerigar, or budgie for short (the origin of this name is discussed in Chapter nine).

This book aims to introduce the budgerigar to the American public as a tame, talking friend and companion which is kept single. Only a budgerigar which is kept alone and away from all other birds will learn to talk and become an affectionate pet. If he has no mate in his cage, he will become very much attached to his master and other members of the family. With his cage door open, he will fly in and out, follow his master about the house, perch on his finger when called, help with sewing, writing, knitting, and even cooking and washing dishes. He likes to get under the faucet and be sprayed, probably thinking himself in the jungle or on the plains of Australia during a nice tropical rain. Suddenly he may start talking, bob his head and say all the little phrases he has been taught—even some lengthy sentences. Then off he goes; without any warning he flies with lightning speed all though the house or around a number of corners to his favorite resting place before a mirror. Here he will admire himself, kiss his reflection, talk to himself, or suddenly imitate the wild bird calls and melodies that have been whistled to him. At times he will be very quiet and affectionate, and for a long time will sit cuddled under your chin or against you cheek, taking a nap when you do. But do not depend upon him to let you sleep. Suddenly he may become mischievous and give you a little nip in the ear lobe to see what will happen, or he may investigate all the buttons on your clothing and try hard to dislodge them. In brief, he is an active little bird which will brighten a quiet house with his constant cheer and exuberant joy of living.

It may prove of special interest to insert at this point some biographical notes on individual budgerigars. Each bird is different and has his own personality. Breeders or trainers who have taught several of these birds to talk and who have used indentical methods in taming and teaching each bird have observed how widely these pets vary in behavior and in the speed with which they will learn.

There is Jackie in Wisconsin. It took him fully six months before he said: "Hello Jackie, nice bird." The family waited impatiently and repeated these words tirelessly with no response from the bird for a long time. It is hard to say what caused this delay. Possibly the different voices of the children confused the young budgie. One day the daughter of the house removed all playthings and toys from the cage, thinking the bird was playing too hard and listening too little. Two days later the bird said the above phrase for the first time. Now he is a veteran talker.

Another Jacky, in Chicago, was not very friendly at first. He would fly to the chandelier and sit there for hours. When a T-stick was pushed against his breast, he did not want to step on it. The T-stick was then pushed against him with increasing pressure, but Jacky could not be forced to loosen his grip on the bar of the chandelier. He pressed with all his might against the stick until the whole chandelier was pushed sideways. He was a very strong and determined little budgie, and a very reserved one. When four months old, he suddenly became friendly and at the same time learned to say his name. He developed into a large and beautiful bird, a very clear talker and a most affectionate pet. Now he takes naps when his owner does, sits on her shoulder and never awakens her. When his owner looks at him through half-closed eyelids, she sees Jacky sitting there with closed eyes. At present Jacky is more than two years old and his owner would never think of leaving him behind when going on a trip. Jacky has his own little traveling cage and has taken trips to California, Kansas, and New York. He definitely does not like to look out of the window when the train is in motion and he does not like to be rocked too much. One night the train shook more than usual, and this caused Jacky to scold all night long, keeping his owner awake. On the other trips he behaved perfectly and did not seem to feel strange in a new house. At home he is kept in the same room with a singing canary and often flies on top of the canary cage for a visit. He even has learned a few calls from the canary's song. He was one year old and already an accomplished talker when the canary was allowed to be in the same room with him. The presence of the canary has neither interfered with his talking nor kept him from learning more words, and has not diminished his affection for the members of the family.

Bobby is a budgie with a strong personality. He grew up together with a baby squirrel monkey. Bobby was tame and affectionate from the first and said his name when barely three months old. He rapidly learned more words and phrases and never copied the various sounds of the monkey. When six months old, he could say clearly and without mistakes: "Bobby, nice Bobby. Want a kiss? (with two kissing sounds following it). Bobby is just precious. Thank you very much. Talk to me, honey." He and the

A nice playpen equipped with a "gym" will assist you in training your budgie to do tricks and will provide both pet and owner with hours of fun.

monkey played hide and seek around the owner's neck, the monkey trying to grab the bird from behind and the bird trying to pinch the monkey's tail. The monkey had learned never to approach the bird from the front. Whenever he tried to, the bird would give his hands a sharp jab. Bobby certainly could stand his ground. He only needed to move his head suddenly, indicating he was on the alert and ready to bite, and the monkey would retreat in great haste. Bobby's coat of feathers is of a fine pastel shade with a white head, faint gray wing-markings on a white ground, and a delicate blue on breast and rump. Now he is kept in a room of pastel colors and makes a beautiful picture sitting before the mirror among the creams and pinks and light blues constituting the color scheme of the room.

There is Tuffy who makes life miserable for Tilly, the dachshund. Tuffy approaches the sleeping dog and, without provocation, bites his tail. Tilly jumps up and whirls around. Tuffy bites hard into the nose of the approaching dog. The dog runs away in mortal terror. Fear is something Tuffy does not know.

And then there is Budgie, who occasionally enjoys a fight with a Siamese fighting fish. The ferocious little fish comes to the glass wall of the tropical fish aquarium while Budgie approaches the same spot from the outside and, with feathers raised, attacks his opponent by hammering against the glass. The fish, unafraid and determined, goes after the hooked beak which annoys him through the glass. Back and forth they go, time and again. Budgie's master only hopes the glass wall separating the two combatants will not wear thin.

Tony likes the two spaniels in his house. He flies to their heads and backs. The dogs never harm the little bird, nor does the bird bite the dogs. He merely cuddles into their long hair to keep warm. When Tony goes for a walk on the floor, the dogs may come and gently sniff at him and then walk off. All three are peaceful companions.

Tiny Tim can whistle the "Star Spangled Banner." Cobalt blue Peter Pan is kept in a room decorated in blue and rose. And then there are Perry, Jerry, Cupie, Tricksy, Skipper, Topper, Peter, Cockie, Terry, Dew Drop, Pancho, Benny, Woody, Dickie, Philip, Doc, Mr. Poo, Sir Keeto and many more, each with his own accomplishments, tricks, melodies, words, rhymes, and often

A gray hen, big, bold and steady in the showcage, and a grand worker in the nesting season.

lengthy sentences. For the sake of convenience we have called all pet budgies in this book "he," although *it should definitely be understood that there also are many talented and well-trained female budgies.*

The following are personal histories of four different budgerigars, as described by their respective owners. We shall hear first about Mickey, next Socrates, then Blue Boy, and last about Mucki.

Mister Mickey

We were not overjoyed at the prospect of a little budgerigar. You see, we were not acquainted with these birds. Our budgie came to us when he was six weeks old, and we named him Mickey. He was friendly and companionable from the very beginning, and after twenty-four hours we could not have been persuaded to part with him for any amount of money.

We soon found that he wanted to be with us and to be talked to, so we started in at once repeating his name, also two sentences of four words each. These we repeated several times each day. When he was three months old, he said his name; at three and one-half months he repeated the sentences with ease. After this he learned very quickly.

By the time he was a year old he had acquired a vocabulary of approximately one hundred words, which included long sentences and nursery rhymes:

> Three lines of "Little Jack Horner."
> Two lines of "Hickory, Dickory, Dock."
> Two lines of "Pussy cat, pussy cat."
> And "To be or not to be, that is the question."

Mickey is now over two years old. He repeats a statement after hearing it three or four times. One very interesting feature of his reproduction is that it is so perfect that you can identify the person who has taught him the particular sentence or rhyme he is saying, so that each member of the family gets a special thrill. When he says, "Mickey is a big boy," or "Mickey eats his spinach," he is quite American, but when he says, "Mickey is my precious wee boy," or "Merry Christmas," there is a pronounced Scottish accent.

Candy dislodged the metal mirror from her playstand and delighted in carrying it around.

If you do not like to eat your meals alone, a budgie makes a wonderful companion. He will fly to you with the request, "Talk to me, sweetheart," or say, "Where is the big boy?" so you just can't be lonely or dumpy with a budgie around. In fact he is ever faithful and will learn whatever you are willing to teach him, be it words or games.

Miss J. Scott and Miss E. Hately
Chicago, Illinois

Socrates, the Philosopher

Our budgerigar became a member of our household when he was six weeks old. He seemed such a solemn, wise little fellow that we named him Socrates. We became very fond of him. He was particularly a valuable companion for me because invalidism kept me confined to bed. Unable to read or to indulge in active forms of recreation, I spent much time playing with Socrates and trying to teach him to talk.

In mid-September, when he was four and a half months old, Socrates delighted us by making halting effects to say, "Hello, Socrates." It begin with "Lo teez," and soon developed into clear expression. We expanded our teaching to expressions such as "Nice Bird," "Pretty good," "Pretty good fellow," and a few others.

Once started on the way to broader education, Socrates made rapid progress. He learned to flutter his wings when asked, "Shall we fly?" He knows the meaning of a dozen words and expressions. Lately, when he becomes tired in the evening, he repeats, "Socrates want to go to bed," or "Shall we go to bed?" To say that he really knows the meanings of words would be inaccurate, but certainly he has learned associations of words and activities.

Both my wife and I have experimental urges. We have selected phrases that were difficult just to find out if our little bird could really learn them. The results have amazed us. Socrates can speak clearly when he chooses and can say almost a hundred and fifty separate words. He learned them in phrases and sentences such as these:

An exhibition budgie showing a set of nicely spaced, large and desirable spots. The necklace is the crowning glory of the show bird and. . . why not keep a bird that is beautiful and a good pet at the same time?

Socrates is a philosopher.

Socrates is a pretty good fellow.

This is a preposterous situation.

It's terrible, the way the rising generation is going to the
  dogs!

That is the proper procedure.

To be or not to be, that is the question.

I'm a surprising parrakeet.

If wishes were horses, beggars would ride.

"The time has come, the walrus said.

To speak of many things;

Of shoes, and ships, and sealing wax.

Of cabbages and kings."

I am in a terrible predicament.

He still has difficulty with sealing wax, but that is the only word
he has stumbled on for long.

These expressions are not always repeated as learned. It seems
that Socrates is also fond of experimenting. He makes up combinations that suit his fancy. While I write this he is saying, "Peter
Piper pickled peppers if wishes beggars." He finishes with a kissing sound and, "Want a kiss?" This jumbling of words and
phrases does not seem to interfere with correct repetition of what
he has learned. Perhaps these made-up expressions are merely a
form of play, for, when he chooses, Socrates will go through a list
of statements correctly.

However, it is not only his ability to talk that makes a budgie a
lovable pet. His presence is always cheering and his activities
always interesting. For example, Socrates flies from room to room
visiting mirrors. Without the whir of wings and the flash of turquoise, our apartment would seem dull indeed.

Mr. L.E. Schlytter
Chicago, Illinois

Blue Boy

What a thrill it was the day "Pretty Blue Boy" introduced
himself to us by his own name in his unmistakable voice! He was
just four months old. From that very day he ceased to be just a
bird—he became a real little personality, an actual member of the
household of seven.

Blue Boy came to live with us at the age of six weeks. Every one of us loved him from the very first and he loved every one of us. The confidence he felt in us was unbelievable. He would hop on any finger thrust gently and slowly into his cage. By the end of the first week he would sit quietly and confidently on any finger and listen as we spoke his name over and over, slowly and distinctly. Nor was it long before he would fly across the room and perch on a finger when he was called, and imitate the sound of a kiss.

Every day, and many times a day, we made it a business of letting Blue Boy out of his cage and playing with him—never neglecting the many quiet moments when we tried to teach him his name. This never became monotonous, for, though we were anxiously awaiting the eventful day when he would really talk to us, he was such an interesting playmate that he kept us constantly amused with his new and cunning tricks.

After the first few weeks, Blue Boy was seldom in his cage, for he spent hours on his special little playground which we made for him. Here he kept busy with his ladders, bars, bells, swings, perches of various heights, a feeding station, and a fair-sized mirror before which he spent much time prancing and strutting.

Blue Boy is now fourteen years old. He is continually adding to his repertoire of cunning tricks, and his vocabulary is growing beyond all our expectations. At present there are more than three hundred words, any one of which is clearly understood by any guest in the home. We who are always with him recognize many more words which he occasionally weaves into his own musical bird chatter.

As Blue Boy grows a bit older we notice he learns new words in a much shorter time. While we waited three months to hear his first words (his name), it is not unusual now to hear him at the end of a week repeating something we have been teaching him. And most amazing of all is when he says things we have not actually taught him. For instance, his two favorite expressions are, "Talk to me," and "Can you say that?" Doubtless we have said these words to him many times without a thought of teaching.

"Does the bird really talk, or are you just like fond parents who imagine they hear something in the baby's first babblings?" This is a common question asked by many of our friends. But after one

14

A beautiful young bird. When about 30 days old, young budgies begin to leave the nest. It is best to keep them with the parents for another eight to ten days. At the end of that period, it is advisable to separate them and place the chicks in a separate cage and start training.

visit when they hear and see Blue Boy they become enthusiastic boosters and all will verify the following vocabulary:

Pretty Blue Boy. Good-bye, Juanita. O.K.
Little Blue Boy can say that, of course he can.
Hello, everybody.
Blue Boy is just beautiful.
He's a precious little rascal.
What are you doing? Playing gin rummy?
I want to talk to Louise. I want to kiss Louise.
Puddy is a good doggie, but he can't talk.
Poor little Socrates, he's lost, he flew away, way up high.
Tst, tst, tst, isn't that too bad.
Dirty, dirty, oh so dirty.
Hello Blanche, I love you. Hello Sweetheart.
I'm a little budgie from Australia.
Talk to me, Nettie B. Kiss me.
Merry Christmas. Happy New Year.
I'm a very good little boy.
Lutie came on choo choo from California.

A report of Blue Boy's accomplishments would not be complete without some mention of his entertaining tricks.

The card table and cards mean just one thing to Blue Boy. He hops on the table, jumps up and down, picks up the cards, and runs to the edge and drops them on the floor, and then says with much expression, "Naughty Blue Boy. Naughty Blue Boy. You little rascal. You little fat rascal."

Polished fingernails are his delight. He kisses them and says, "Kiss me, kiss me; make it smack, like that."

Just eat a piece of bread in Blue Boy's presence and that is the signal for him to perch on your shoulder and steal a wee bit. It is a surprising sight for Blue Boy's guests to see him nibbling from the same tiny bite of bread with "Puddles," the big springer spaniel of whom he has no fear.

He loves to sit on top of the newspaper or on a book when we are reading and say over and over again, "Talk to me. Come here and talk to me." And mirrors are his special delight. He sits for hours and talks to the other bird in the mirror. Here is where we hear him practicing all his vocabulary. And he always shares his lettuce or some special treat with the little reflection.

Blue Boy was our first budgie and naturally we thought he was unusual. However, it is our firm belief that his interesting personality is the direct result of the untiring and conscientious effort of every member of the family. This belief has found support through the training of four other tame budgerigars, each one of which turned out an excellent talker and with a distinct and individual personality.

Juanita Stapp
Chicago, Illinois

Mucki, the Linguist

I had to leave my tame and talking lovebird back in Germany, and must confess that I have been more homesick for that infinitesimal speck of blue and white than for anything else I had to leave there. My memories of my little budgerigar, Bubi, are manifold. I only have to close my eyes to recall a sweet little boy's face looking up at me with a doubtful expression, mixed with hidden reproach, because I decided that it would be too dangerous for Bubi to undertake a boat trip in the bathtub. A new track part or another tunnel for our toy railroad usually was required to restore mutual confidence. I can still see all those railway tracks running through my room and out into the hall, into my landlady's bedroom, and finally all over the apartment. I see Bubi traveling on the train, wings flapping happily, ducking for one tunnel, and jumping over another, calling out stations while the boy in a shrill voice tries to explain that the needle-point chair represents Paris, the green one Munich, and that Venice is under the kitchen sink. And there is my landlady again, arms akimbo like a Boston-bean-pot, trying to give her kind face a severe expression to underline her argument—"Listen Miss, I rented one room to you—Look at that mess!"

I never knew exactly what I answered on such occasions until Bubi surprised us with saying: "Go on, you could not do without that bird any more, and you know it too!"

Thus ended the most successful fight for LEBENSRAUM that has ever been fought with a complete victory for the budgie and satisfaction for everyone concerned.

Budgies love noise. The plastic pool catches the marbles. At other times the pool is filled with water and greens are placed into it for a budgie bath.

"Bubi is well," wrote Mrs. G. in her last letter, "I could not do without him anymore, and I just wonder how you can."

This started me on my search throughout the city for another tame lovebird that would learn to talk. It took me a long time to find Mrs. K., who was the first one in the U.S.A. who has made a hobby of raising them successfully for talking.

Will we ever forget the blessed day on which we came home with a tiny blue feather-ball that in spite of its small size managed to confiscate all my attention for the next few months! I cooked short dinners and neglected my house, I even looked on smilingly when that cute little rascal chewed up my favorite plants. I manufactured a gymnasium set with swings and a ring and bells hanging temptingly everywhere. From morning till night I did my best to get the bird interested in his toys. It may sound silly, but even during the night I was engrossed in this serious business. I had nightmares. I dreamed that I had forgotten to give him water and to blow out the shells from his seeds and that I found my poor little Muckie (pronounced Mookey) starved to death in front of an apparently well-filled feed cup, which actually contained nothing but empty hulls. Yes, *little* Muckie was a *big* worry for the first few weeks, though an extremely cute one. In a way he still is, for his frantic desire to love and be loved has not diminished, and he still is sad and acts very much hurt when we leave him alone for awhile. But now he begins to pay me for my troubles by getting more intelligent every day. He speaks English, German, and Spanish. He can say "Hello Mucki, how do you do? Mucki is beautiful, Muckie es muy bonito, Good night, Good morning, Mucki ist sehr muede, Oh du kleiner Mucki du! Take a trip, go to Oshkosh," etc. His permanent vocabulary consists of about fity words. It would be larger if we were more systematic. We should stick to one sentence until he masters it completely. Without really intending to, we present him with too large a vocabulary at one time. That probably explains his surprising us sometimes by reciting a sentence such as, "Now where is that cracker box again!" or "Look, Mucki, the pigeons are here." But he cannot be persuaded to repeat such a sentence the second time.

At present Mucki sings the first line of a cradle song pretty successfully, and we are almost sure that he will be able to sing it all, in about a year.

Mucki loves to ride on a toy automobile and he will be presented with a race track on his first birthday, mostly to make things more convenient for me, who has to watch that he does not bump against furniture or walls and thus lose interest. He also loves to crawl through a tunnel of empty yarn rolls, ringing a bell at the exit while emerging. He loves bells. He has some bells fittingly adorned with blue and pink bow-ties in his drawer together with some jacks (mostly broken), a bobbypin threaded with yellow yarn not long enough to become dangerous, a shining penny, etc.

Every morning he pulls out his drawer to get out his treasures, chatting excitedly. He has a bowling alley on a window-sill, without pins but with plenty of pretty marbles to roll back and forth. A shallow baking pan was converted into a pool-table, and a marble in the lid of a little sewing-basket invites him to waltz round and round time and again. Then there are the pebbles in the flower pots. He loves to carry them to the top of his gymnasium set and from there drop them into his empty bathtub. They make such a lovely noise. These hobbies and many others that Mucki acquired give me a chance to do my knitting without having him constantly on the end of one of the needles, bobbing up and down joyously.

For quite a while we were entirely unaware of Mucki's meat-eating tendencies and kept him carefully away from the meat on our dinner plates, fearing that meat would impair his health. We changed our opinion after we had an opportunity to watch him on his first hunting trip after a delectable, fat fly. You should have seen him licking his beak, making sure that not a crisp leg got lost. Mucki loves roast beef. And how his eyes roll and sparkle with a gourmet's delight when he works on a chicken bone three times as big as he is!

Holes were punched into the table tennis ball so that the budgie could to put his toes into them.

Budgie says, "He loves me, he loves me not," each time he pushes the table tennis ball.

Before I close, I must tell that Mucki has a special talent for getting into trouble. In the short span of his life he has already had three narrow escapes. Once he almost drowned in the bathtub. That taught us not to have water around or other liquids deep enough for him to drown in. Another time he nearly choked on a nutshell splinter. This was an extraordinary accident which probably won't happen a second time, as he has grown older and more experienced. On another occasion he got hold of a hairnet. I never witnessed such an entanglement. He had worked it so completely under his plumage that we could not see it at all. I discovered it while fumbling around to find the cause of his death (because dead he seemed). Well, we managed to cut it off in time and had the joy of seeing our tiny sky-blue bundle of loveliness revive. We hope that this will be his last frightful experience so that we will be able to enjoy his amiable, teasing, Peter Pan existence for many years to come.

At present we are very grateful to have all the doors secured with doorstops, for Mucki's latest habit is to sit on top of a door, watching the world below in utter contentment. He certainly keeps our brains busy and our minds off our troubles.

Mrs. G.F. Riss
Chicago, Illinois

A Phenomenal Pet

Those who have never had a very tame budgie in the house will not believe it possible for such a small bird to be taken so fully into the human heart. Many a tame budgie is a member of the family in the true sense of the word. The bird takes part in family life and is an unending source of amusement. He has a sense of time. When the master of the house returns home at night and the bird hears the key turn in the lock, he calls loudly, "Daddy, Daddy," then lands on his shoulder as soon as daddy has entered. He will call each member of the family by name, never making a mistake. When mother writes at her desk, he walks over the paper she is writing on and tries to pick up the words and letters. He romps with the children on the floor and often dances while reciting some of the phrases he has learned. This is a comical sight, his legs being very short.

Often the budgie gets in the way and is scolded. Soon he will scold himself in the same annoyed voice and nobody can be angry with him. He has to be there when someone is telephoning, climbing into the mouthpiece and warbling and talking, making the telephone conversation very difficult.

Budgies like to have their heads and cheeks scratched. One budgie will hook his beak under a fingernail, lift the finger, then push his head under the finger—an invitation to be scratched.

Another budgie, living in a country home, has learned many calls of the wild birds. When the outdoor birds come to the feeding station close to the window, the budgie calls them in their own language. On several occasions, when a bird of another species was brought into the house, the budgie tried out all the wild bird calls until he received an answer from the newcomer. Often he uses human language, and if that does not work, he will just laugh, "Ha, ha, ha."

One budgie, a close friend of a hunting dog, a pointer, often crawls into the dog's mouth until the good-natured dog practically spits him out. Touching friendships have developed between budgies and dogs, especially when the dogs are patient. Budgies are great teasers and often nip a dog on the tail or feet. The pointer we just mentioned often puts a stop to this by placing his big paw right on top of the budgie. With a loud shriek the bird then flies away and leaves the dog in peace for awhile.

Only a budgie who is taken into the home very young, when about six weeks of age, and who is played with frequently during the first few weeks, will make an adorable pet. A bird left to

It is very common for a pet budgie to sit in front of a mirror and talk to itself. During this conversation, the bird may regurgitate food. This is perfectly normal. Budgerigar parents feed their babies with food that they regurgitate from their crops. Your pet budgie is just trying to be friendly and feed the image in the mirror.

himself a great deal of the time is likely to become lonely, dull, and unresponsive.

It is surprising, however, that some owners who are at work all day have nevertheless made a sucess of teaching their budgie to talk and to become an affectionate pet. In fact, they often are more successful than housewives who are at home most of the time and postpone training and talking lessons. People who have to go to work usually concentrate on teaching their pets during morning and evening hours and on weekends. Some exceedingly well-trained birds are the proud possessions of "working girls." When a bird has to be left alone during the day, a mirror and his toys will keep him company. At times a baby budgie may become too attached to the bird in the mirror or to his cage. In that case both mirror and cage should be removed or covered with a cloth while his master is home and wishes to play with the bird and train him. Many advise that a mirror be kept near a bird so he will not become too lonesome when left to himself. Others believe that a mirror near a baby budgie will ruin him as a potential pet and talker because the little budgie will become attached to the bird in the mirror instead of his owner and as a consequence will not develop into an affectionate companion who is eager to copy the words of his master.

When training a young budgie, we ourself have never covered the mirrors in the house. We never had trouble in teaching to talk even if between lessons the bird sat often in front of the mirror on his playstand. Many budgies have become outstanding talkers and the best of pets with mirrors about at all times. On the other hand, if a bird is left too much to himself and does not receive affection and proper care, he will become lonely and unhappy or even sick. His only friend then seems to be the bird in the mirror. He will become attached to it and prefer its company to that of people.

It seems advisable to cover mirrors for the first few weeks after a new baby budgie has arrived in the home. When the bird has become thoroughly tame and begins to come to his master volun-

Many birds are naturally good-natured and take very readily to training. A pet budgie will teach itself many cute little tricks or learn them with some encouragement from you!

A budgie learns by association of ideas. It will also react to the kind of treatment it receives. If you are gentle from the beginning you will have a gentle bird; if you are rough or teasing, your pet may develop into a biting, noisy and disobedient budgie.

tarily, the presence of mirrors in the room will do no harm. When the little budgie becomes mature, he will attempt to feed the bird in the mirror with a whitish fluid from his crop (crop milk) and occasionally with regurgitated seeds; as a result mirrors will have to be cleaned frequently. Many a pet budgie which had escaped into the open has been coaxed back to the shoulder of his master or into his cage by being shown his beloved mirror.

It is indeed amazing that a bird as small as a budgie is able to learn to talk so easily. We know of pet budgies who can say several hundred words. Such birds sometimes start off with one phrase and finish with another, thus changing the meaning. The budgie-made combinations of words and phrases often sound more intriguing than the sentences that the birds were taught.

Someone not familiar with tame budgies will not readily believe the many examples of courage and fearlessness observed in their behavior. At one time a baby grackle which had fallen out of the nest was brought home. We fed the helpless creature; it was soon quite large and with its long bill began to tease the budgies. These budgies, untamed birds of all ages, were afraid of the big black bird. Our tame pet, however, thought nothing of attacking the grackle; he nipped it in the feet and finally chased it. The grackle knew when it was licked and kept at a safe distance from then on. The grackle was later given its liberty.

Budgies can become very angry too. Once we boarded a pet, an Opaline Cobalt, at the house of friends while we went away on a trip. We had placed a bag containing seeds on the bottom of his cage. When the cover was taken off in his foster home, our pet saw the unfamiliar bag of seeds. This angered him and he scolded loudly and punched his bell viciously, with feathers raised like a fighting cock. This excitement did not pass until the seed bag was removed. Our friends were shocked at this display of temper; they had intended to shower the bird with love and kindness so he would not pine for us.

At night our pet is placed into a large closet. We try not to enter the closet later in the evening, but when we have to do so, we speak softly to the bird so that he will not become frightened. However, he does not take kindly to being awakened; we usually get a scolding.

In this connection it should be stressed that one never should scold a budgie. He will notice the disapproval in the voice, but he will not, of course, understand the "reason why." The scolding will merely intimidate him and make training more difficult. An adult budgie does not mind being scolded; he is quite bold and will think it funny. Other kinds of punishment such as slapping on the wings or beak or being angry with the bird are strictly taboo at all times. He cannot be made to feel badly (like a dog), but may become ill-tempered and bite. Any misconduct will have to be ignored.

An accomplished talker with more than one hundred words in his vocabulary will not say constantly all he has learned. He will choose the phrases he likes best and those he learned last. If his vocabulary is kept up by the owner who repeats the old phrases,

Start your pet's training by slowly putting your finger into the cage. Talk gently to the bird. Slowly move your finger so as to stroke the breast of your budgie. Then, moving extremely slowly, place your forefinger under its chest, just in front of the place where the legs join the body. By gentle lifting, the budgie will step up on your finger to regain its balance. Hold your finger very still and keep talking all the time (it does not matter what you say).

the bird will say them occasionally, but will also remain interested in learning new sentences. Even though some of the earliest phrases he has learned are not repeated to him, he may suddenly come out and say one which he has not heard for months. One bird surprised the family by repeating a phrase he had learned two years before and which had not been repeated to him during that time.

Budgerigars will recognize persons, but there is not uniformity in their expressions or preference. Some young budgies will fly to no one but the person who cares for them. Others are very vain. These seemingly want to make an impression on everyone. When company comes, a bird of this type will neglect the family and make up to the guests. Often a budgie will not pay any attention all evening to his mistress who has been about most of the day, but will concentrate all his affection upon the husband just home from work. A colored maid had made friends with a budgie and the bird frequently flew to her. After a while this maid left and her place was taken by another colored maid, similar in appearance. Yet for some reason, the bird never went near this second maid.

Budgerigars also remember the circumstances under which phrases have been taught them. "Blue Boy" says, "Naughty Blue Boy" many times when he is on the card table, disturbing the playing cards. "Socrates" often says, "Want to go to bed?" in the evening when he is getting sleepy. One night, with company present and his bed time long past, he flew to his owner's shoulder and said over and over again, "Want to go to bed?" until finally attention was given him and he was put in his cage in a dark room and covered up for the night. "Jacky" always says a certain phrase to the man of the house who taught him this particular phrase. Another budgie says, "No, no," when he takes part in the owner's letter-writing by perching on the fountain pen.

Not only will budgerigars remember phrases and persons, but they also have a good memory for places. For example, a budgerigar having been away from home for many months will, upon his return, immediately fly to the perching places that were his favorite before his trip.

It is of interest that budgerigars and other members of the parrot family have a larger brain in relation to their body weight than other birds.

II Housing

The housing problem for the new little budgie that is going to be taught to talk is a very simple one. The most widely used type of cage is chromium plated; it is practical and easily cleaned. There are a few enameled cages of different colors offered on the market. Any bird of the parrot family kept confined in a painted cage will chew and gnaw on the wires and an enameled cage will soon look chipped. However, where a pet budgie spends the greater part of the day on his playstand, a red, yellow, white, blue or green painted cage is very pretty and will not seriously be damaged for several years. Many an artistic owner has worked out his individual color scheme, selecting a budgerigar of the shade to match the room in which he is going to be kept and using a painted cage of the color which would set off that of the bird and show him to his best advantage. For this purpose a cage would have to be painted at home with special care, using leadless enamel paint and applying it very evenly. Warning must be given not to poison a bird by using a freshly painted cage. In order to avoid having the artistic effect spoiled by a cage with the paint peeled off and wire showing in places, it is advisable to keep two cages for a bird, repainting one while the other is in use and allowing at least four weeks for drying.

Although budgies do not throw seeds around as many other birds do, a screen, plastic, or glass guard will keep the hulls and sand inside the cage. There are cages with inside cups and others with outside cups. It takes the baby budgie a little longer to learn to eat out of an outside cup but, after he has once found it, it will serve its purpose as well as an inside cup. In general, outside cups are smaller and have to be refilled more often. They should be made of glass because porcelain cups do not let the light through for the birds to see the seeds.

Cage covers may be obtained to fit the cage—also seed catchers which will catch any hulls or feathers blown out of the cage when the bird is using his wings. If there is any danger of draft or if the bird is expected to go to sleep in a lighted room, a heavier cover is often necessary. Any cloth, piece of blanket, or turkish towel may be used. If a gap is left in the cover on the side toward the wall, the bird will have enough air.

Handsome cage covers have been designed. One is made of ermine lined with turquoise blue silk. Another is made of quilted silk decorated with silk bows. Still another cover is beautifully hand-embroidered with the name of the parrakeet stitched on the outside. Some of these elaborate covers are fitted with a second cover made of plastic material to protect the bird against wind when carried out of the house to a car and back.

When a metal cage has been purchased, it must be thoroughly washed with hot water, because metal cages receive an acid wash before leaving the factory. Have the cage completely dry before placing the bird in it. Put a piece of paper on the bottom of the cage. This can be cut to fit, or else papers the size of the cage drawer with sand glued on can be purchased. However, a good grit mixture should be kept in a treat cup because the glued-on sand is hard to pick off and shreds of paper are likely to come off with the sand. The bird, in this way, will eat only an insufficient amount of grit (see Chapter three, under Gravel). The papers can easily be replaced by clean ones daily or a few times weekly, depending on how much time the bird spends inside his cage.

Unusual Cages

It is well known how extemely fond owners of a single tame budgie may become of their pet. Such persons may spare neither expense nor effort to obtain an especially beautiful cage for their bird, yet finding such a cage may prove very difficult. We know of many people who have gone shopping in all the bird stores and antique shops not only of one but of many large cities in order to acquire a cage of unusual design for their unusual pet.

Cages of antique design are probably more sought after than any other kind of unusual cage. Many people have antique furniture in their homes and modern cages do not fit into rooms panelled with dark wood or furnished with period chairs, oriental rugs, or drapes of subdued color.

Cages with wrought iron stands used to be on the American market. We know of one such cage measuring two and a half feet in length which has a little roof garden for plants and a large

A picturesque early American cage.

sliding door of glass. The stand, too, has provisions for potted plants. The owner proudly relates that she paid one hundred twenty-five dollars for cage and stand and that she would not part with the little pet budgie inside even for a thousand dollars.

Cages of early American design have turned wooden posts of maple at each corner, made in the manner of the old four-poster beds. The wooden framework is screwed on from the outside and cannot be attacked by a budgie. Stands for these cages consist of one large post supporting the platform on which the cage rests. The post branches into three lathe-turned legs.

Box-type log cabin cages are designed for open porches. Except for the front they are made of solid miniature logs and protect birds from too much sun or wind and rain outside.

Cages of Spanish design with their framework and stands made of wrought iron are very attractive indeed. One such cage we have seen was four feet long and had a back wall of solid wood on which landscape was painted. The roof had three gables in a row, each adorned with an imitation window with a little balcony, all decorated with wire loops of a design resembling wrought iron. Under each window was a door with an ornamental arch above. Metal stairs with a railing in a wrought iron design led up to each door. There was a porch at either end of the cage accommodating feeding, water, and bathing dishes. This cage had no stand but was hung on a wall. Several budgerigars of special beauty occupying this Spanish mansion had done no harm to the painting since a coat of varnish adequately protected it against attack.

Cages of Swiss design are usually smaller and have one gable with wooden beams crossing at the top and ending in a carved design which often represents horses' head. One pattern has a hand-carved bird with open wings at the top. Budgerigars can easily be kept in a cage with woodwork on the outside and out of reach of their beaks. Smooth wooden walls also are not attacked by budgerigars. Many Swiss-type cages have three walls of solid wood with only the front supplied with wires; they are meant to be hung outdoors on nice days to allow the bird the enjoyment of outdoor air and at the same time protecting him from too much sun and wind.

Oriental cages of ancient design are sometimes seen on exhibition. For example, three cages collected in China by Berthold Laufer in 1923 are displayed in the Chicago Museum of Natural History. One of these was made during the Kien-Lung period (1736-95) and is decorated with seventeen hand-carved ivory ornaments and figures of the Eight Immortals. A small, shallow bird bath of amber is centrally mounted on a stem also carved from amber. The feet are carved ivory roses. The second cage is entirely carved of ivory; its perches are mounted on carved ivory roses and its colorful food and water cups are made of metal with painted

The wild budgerigar, *Melopsittacus undulatus,* is the best known of the 52 psittacines from Australia. It inhabits the arid interior.

A domesticated budgie and its mirror.

There are a number of cages on the market made especially for budgerigars; such cages have horizontal bars. Large canary cages having close-set bars also can be used, but budgie owners should try to obtain cages designed for budgerigars. Pet shops selling bird supplies normally carry a wide selection of cages and can provide good advice about the advantages and disadvantages of each type.

enamel designs; its door can be pushed up and down and stays at any point. The third cage, with two ivory cups inside, is decorated with carved foliage and plum blossoms. It is suspended by a metal hook of beautiful design and attached to a plaque which is damascened with a pattern in gold.

A period bird cage copied from a Louis XV antique design is manufactured in America today. It measures thirty-six inches high, twenty-eight wide and eleven inches deep, is hand carved and obtainable in bleached wood or painted finishes. The cost is approximately two hundred seventy-five dollars at the time of this writing. It may be placed on a table or on a bracket that can be purchased with it. The latter is designed to be screwed to a wall; it is hand-carved, matching the cage, and is offered for about ninety dollars. A hand-made smaller cage with mahogany framework and roof may be ordered for approximately three hundred sixty dollars. It may be ordered mounted on one end of a handsome mahogany coffee table; the combination of table and cage will cost about seven hundred twenty-five dollars.

A large mahogany cage with hand-turned posts and hand-carved reinforcements between posts and hand-turned wooden ornaments on top of each post may be made to order. It is seventy inches high, forty-two inches wide and fifteen inches deep. With mahogany table it sells for about six hundred ninety-five dollars.

A picture frame cage may be ordered in a variety of patterns to match any style of room. It is available in French provincial, modern, wormy chestnut, combed woods, and antiqued. It measures sixteen by sixteen inches, nine inches deep, and can be recessed into a wall or hung flush on a wall. It sells for forty-five to fifty-five dollars at the time of this writing.

Picture frame cage. Designed by John R. Vail, the cage was made from a sixteen-inch-square frame. The cage is nine inches deep.

A number of birds have the habit of talking only baby talk or their own bird language when looking into the mirror.

A playground affords a means of keeping a budgie happily occupied.

The toys you choose for your budgies should be made of non-toxic materials. Pet shops have a wide variety of toys designed specifically for use by budgies.

The "acoustic" cage; it amplifies a budgie's talking voice.

An "acoustic" cage has been made to amplify the talking voice of a budgie. Such a cage may be made of either wood or metal with the base eighteen inches wide. It is not on the market today so far as we know. Any cage, however, may be made to order if expense does not play a role.

Besides the popular chrome plated cages of various designs (from twenty dollars up)* there are bronze, brass, black, silver, red, blue, and green ones on the market made of solid anodized aluminum bars which resist any attack by the beak of a budgie. Your pet shop may carry or order them for you.

Traveling Cages

In most instances it is not advisable to transport your budgie in his own cage. It usually is too large and heavy and does not protect the bird from draft. If it has to be used, be sure to cover it up

Prices listed in this book are of course simply approximations; prices can vary widely from area to area and time to time.

well and to tie the swing to one side so it will not move in transit and injure or scare the bird. Do the same with bells or strings of beads hanging in the cage.

The owner of "Pal" carries her pet back and forth to work every day in a transport cage that can be modified for the weather. Three sides are made of Plexiglas; the fourth side consists of a screen door for summer or a door of Plexiglas for cool weather. Ven-

Traveling cage; the panel fits on pegs in front of wires.

A treat much relished by a budgie is spray millet. This type millet is not threshed; the seeds are still on the head, and the budgies delight in climbing over the sprays, shelling and eating the seeds.

tilation is supplied by means of holes drilled into the wooden cage top. Pal loves his transport cage. When time comes to go home, he will sit in his little traveling cage waiting to have the door closed and to be taken down the street where children are waiting to keep him company on the way home.

The bird shown here was a very strong and determined little budgie, but a very reserved one. When four months old, though, he suddenly became friendly and at the same time learned to say his name.

For cross-country travel a larger cage is more suitable. The cover lying before the cage may be mounted in front of the wires. It fits into pegs and may be locked above with a key. Two round holes protected by wire screen from the inside admit light and air. The tray at the bottom is covered with wire netting which prevents the bird from stepping into water which may have spilled. The water cup is partially covered with metal to prevent spilling as much as possible.

We hope that before long both types of traveling cages will be manufactured and offered for sale in pet shops.

Cleaning the Cage

Once a week the cage should be thoroughly cleaned. Remove bottom and cups and wash them with soap and water and scrape perches. Once a month allow hot water to run over the cage into all corners; allow it to dry thoroughly on a radiator or in the sun. At this time the perches, too, should receive a good scrubbing with soap and water and be rinsed with boiling water. Red mites, which are at times present when cages are not kept clean, will breed in the crevices at the end of perches. It is important that the perches be thoroughly dried before the bird is allowed to sit on them. Damp perches are injurious to a bird's health. The cage cover also should be washed and the stand wiped thoroughly. Cleanliness is essential to the prevention of disease.

III Feeding

Among birds there are insect-eaters and seed-eaters. Insect-eaters require a great deal of care as regards feeding, while seed-eaters are easily fed and budgerigars especially are very frugal in their eating habits. Wild budgerigars in Australia subsist mainly on grass seeds while in captivity they thrive on millet and canary seeds. When purchasing a baby bird, it is important to feed him the same mixture he is used to. Different breeders and dealers feed slightly varying amounts of each kind of seed. A popular mixture is:

> Four parts large canary seed
> Two parts white Proso millet
> One part oats

A baby bird at first cannot find the seeds in the cup. Plenty of seeds should be on the floor of the cage in a flat dish, such as the

Millet, cuttlefish bone and canary seed are essential nutrients for all budgerigars.

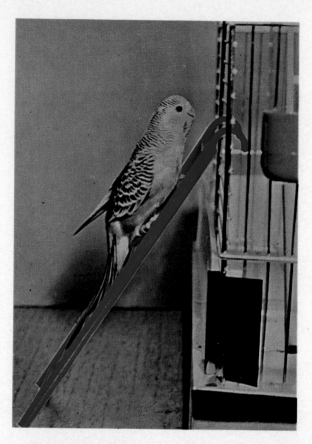

Budgerigars love to
climb, and one of
their favorite toys is a
ladder.

If a budgie likes to talk to a polished fingernail or a shiny ring, putting
him near these attractive objects often can induce him to talk,
especially if his beak is tapped lightly with the fingernail.

cover of a mayonnaise jar. The hulls from the seeds should be blown out every day and the dish should be refilled with seeds. At the same time the seed cup should be kept filled with seeds to overflowing. The bird will learn to find his regular seed cup soon, usually after about a week. After he has eaten several times from the cup, the dish on the cage floor may be removed.

The water cup should be filled with fresh water every day and the cup should be well rinsed. No water needs to be kept on the cage bottom as baby birds drink very little and might step into it and as a consequence catch cold.

Oats are fattening. A growing baby bird needs them, but in summer, when it is very warm, oats should be discontinued. However, in winter, when the house cools a great deal, a few oats daily will help to keep the bird warm. Budgies like oats as much as children like candy. If you want to coax your bird back into the cage, a few oats will usually do the trick. Budgies with their strong beaks are well able to shell whole oats. Steel-cut or hulled oats are found in most mixtures and, if fresh, provide good nourishment.

Canary seed has elongated kernels. Millet varies greatly in quality. It should have plump, round, creamy-colored kernels. Small, dark yellow and red millet, sometimes found in parrakeet mixtures, is meant for finches and is indigestible for budgies. Some seed mixtures sold in bird stores have already been treated with vitamins and minerals. Study the analysis on the label.

All seeds should be kept exposed to the air. They are kept in porous bags, and the seeds should be disturbed occasionally. Seed should never be kept in closed tin boxes. Do not buy more than two pounds at the time for a single budgie and keep these in an open container. Seeds kept in commercial containers may be fed if obtained from bird stores where a fast turnover assures fresh seeds. Otherwise it is better to insist upon seed in bulk, weighed out in the proper proportions. Fresh, sweet seeds will invite worms to grow in them. Frequent stirring of the seeds will prevent the development of cocoons into moths (not clothes moths). Some local stores may carry "Bird Seeds," but these may be seeds for canary birds, entirely unsuited for budgerigars. Even if the package is labeled "Love Bird Mixture" it may be ages old, completely dried up, and best suited to starve a bird to death. Be sure to find a place where you can obtain wholesome seeds of the proper proportions. Care should be taken to keep mice out of bird seeds (see Chapter seven).

It is very important to keep plenty of seeds in the cage at all times. A budgerigar deprived of seeds for twenty-four hours will die. He will also die of starvation if the hulls of the seeds are allowed to accumulate in the seed cup and are mistaken for seeds. Be sure to blow out the hulls every day and replenish the cup with fresh seeds. The hulls from oats are heavy and do not fly out as easily as the hulls from millet and canary seeds. At least once a week all seeds should be thrown out, the cup washed, dried, and refilled with fresh seeds.

Cod-liver Oil

When a young bird is growing out in the wilds, he is exposed to direct and indirect sunshine most of the day. In captivity a substitute for sunshine must be provided in order to prevent the young bird from developing rickets. A budgerigar grows up to the age of one year. If you want to have a large, well-developed bird, you should take the pains to treat a small amount of seeds with cod-liver oil. Any good standard brand of oil may be used. Cod-liver oil should be given all through the year, especially during the dark winter months. This addition to the diet is an absolute necessity, particularly during the molt.

After you have purchased one pound of mixture of millet and canary seeds, put it into a roomy dish. Then add one-half teaspoon of cod-liver oil. Use a measuring spoon so that you will not add too much oil to the seeds. It is better to add too little than too much. An excess of cod-liver oil will make the bird ill. Next mix the oil thoroughly with the seeds. This, too, should be done carefully so that the oil will be distributed evenly. Stir the mixture for some time, then keep it in a cool place. This small amount of seeds treated with cod-liver oil may be kept in a covered jar and placed in the refrigerator. The jar should be washed in soapy water, rinsed and dried before a new batch of treated seeds is put into it. Be sure to wash the seed cup thoroughly with soap and water at least once a week, otherwise the adhering oil will become rancid and will injure the bird's health instead of improving it.

Cod-liver oil may be omitted if the budgie is kept on a screened porch in the summer, because he will be exposed to sunshine

These charming little Australian natives make delightful and decorative pets. Budgerigars, particularly cock birds (as shown), are generally amenable and therefore excellent and colorful additions to your family.

which has not passed through glass. In case a bird is kept inside all summer, cod-liver oil should be given all through the year. This will help prevent overgrown beaks and toenails. On warm days a budgie may be put in an open window in his cage if care is taken not to expose him to hot and glaring sunshine. Have a part of the cage in the shade or cover half of it with a cloth. Most birds prefer indirect sunshine. It must be remembered that these birds are not used to windy weather and may, therefore, easily catch cold.

Budgies love carrots.

Greens

A small piece of fresh, crisp greens should be provided every day. All greens should be washed well before they are given to the bird because they often have been sprayed with poisonous insecticides which adhere to the leaves. Green lettuce is better than the bleached variety. Other greens liked by budgerigars are: green celery leaves, celery stalk cut into one inch pieces, carrot tops, young fresh dandelion and plantain in spring and summer, grated carrots, water cress, spinach, seeding grasses, chickweed, and pieces of apple. Often a young bird does not touch any of these greens, but they should be offered every day. The bird needs the food elements contained in greens for growing and building new feathers. As time goes on the baby bird will start eating greens. If not, the water cup should be removed for two days. Very few birds eat too many greens but, if they do, loose droppings and diarrhea may be the result. In this case, the greens should be taken out of the cage after the bird has eaten some of them. In most cases a bird develops diarrhea from a cold caused by a draft, rather than from greens. Lettuce is more laxative than other greens. Be sure to remove all old and wilted greens from the cage daily.

Some birds will eat lettuce readily, but will not touch any other greens. Nevertheless, a variety should be offered, and the budgie will soon nibble at different greens, especially if he is coaxed a little. Budgerigars seem to be very imitative. A group of them will take to new food more readily than a budgie kept alone. If, in a large flight cage, one bird starts to investigate the new green food, the others will follow suit and soon the whole group will be busy pecking at the unaccustomed greens. A single tame budgie, although he will seldom touch an apple in his cage, will soon nibble on it when he sees his master eat one. Budgerigars like to eat corn on the cob, but this is quite fattening. A bird allowed a great deal of liberty may be permitted more fattening food than one confined to his cage most of the time.

The "Budgie Garden" solves many feeding problems. Ask at your pet shop for one of the containers furnished with seeds which will grow into little plants. Such a garden is placed on or near the playstand and the budgie helps himself to wholesome greens whenever he likes. Or take an inch of root and an inch of green from a carrot, place the piece in half an inch of water until little roots have developed. Then plant it in a flower pot together with some seeds from the budgie mixture. When all have sprouted green leaves, the budgie may enjoy an assortment of fresh

A girl makes a better tutor than a man because she has a higher voice. A man, of course, can teach a bird to talk, but it is desirable that he try to pitch his voice a little higher.

You should provide your budgie with toys while he is still young, because a mature budgie may not show interest in a playground or toys he has never seen before.

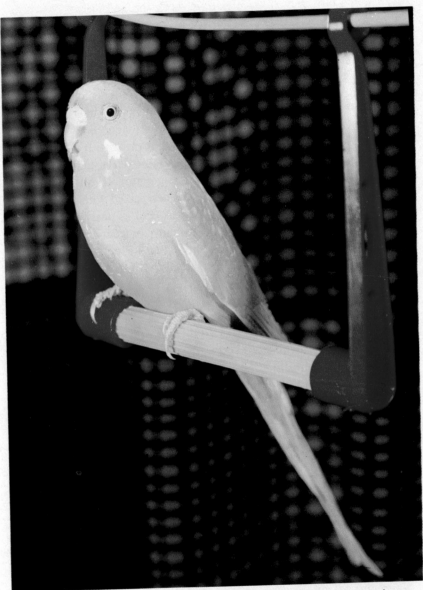

A swing provides endless fun. Various types are offered in pet shops, and budgie owners will derive a great deal of pleasure from selecting different toys.

53

vegetables. If, in additon, gravel has been placed among the green plants, the bird may enjoy picking at both soil and grit.

Greens have vitamin A but consist so largely of water that it is safer to supply another source of this vitamin by the feeding of cod-liver oil. This oil also contains vitamin D, which is very necessary to birds kept indoors. There are no other vitamins in this oil, but its fat content is valuable to those birds which subsist mainly on seeds very low in fat. It is claimed that cod-liver oil will keep fresh indefinitely, but this is not true. Its vitamin A content decreases if the oil is kept exposed to air, heat or light. It is best to obtain a good standard brand from a reputable dealer and keep it tightly covered, preferably in the refrigerator. If allowed to become rancid, it is harmful to birds. When mixed with seeds or other food, the mixture should be kept as cool as possible.

For budgerigars the dosage used by most breeders is one-half teaspoonful cod-liver oil to one pound (two heaping measuring cups) seed. This mixture should be stirred thoroughly to avoid accumulation of oil in clumps of seeds. Any sudden increase of the oil in a bird's food will upset its digestive system. Birds are very sensitive to abrupt changes in diet, and therefore it is not recommended to feed cod-liver oil-treated seeds to birds not used to it without starting them gradually with smaller doses. Birds kept outdoors in the sunshine do not need additional vitamin D, but while breeding indoors they should receive a little cod-liver oil because of the fat, vitamin A and iodine content.

It has been argued that cod-liver oil upsets the livers of young birds in the nest and for this reason should not be fed at that time. If a considerable amount is fed suddenly, cod-liver oil is likely to have this effect, but not if the parent birds are used to it.

It has also been claimed that seeds treated with cod-liver oil turn rancid immediately. This is not true. It takes a long time before

Head study of a young Sky cock. Note the solid thickness and rise of the frontal, the overhang in front over the cere and over the eyes, forming a pronounced brow. Observe the height over the eyes and the rounded sweep into the backskull. Huge, well-spaced spots and the evident proud stance would make this bird outstanding anywhere. This is the kind of head that wins the awards anywhere in the world.

rancidity starts at room temperature. In laboratories it took 300 hours of exposure to an air current of a temperature of 194 degrees Fahrenheit to turn oil rancid.

Any budgie will quickly learn to go up a ladder with rungs one and one-half inches apart.

Gravel

Gravel is an essential in a budgie's diet. He has no teeth, and gravel in the gizzard helps to grind up the seeds. White sand, sold for canaries, is not suitable for budgies. Ask for a coarser gravel (red flint number thirty, granite grit, or ocean sand) mixed with an equal amount of oyster-shell grit. Oyster shell provides some necessary minerals and is beneficial to a bird's digestion. Put the

Budgerigars are well-known all over the world. In 1840, John Gould brought the first living budgie to Europe.

gravel into a treat cup; this is preferable to placing it on the cage floor. Some birds in small cages do not go down on the cage floor and thus are deprived of gravel so necessary to their nutrition. Gravel on the cage floor may get contaminated with droppings. The grit mixture should not contain charcoal because it has been found to rob the bird of vitamins.

Cuttlefish Bone

Cuttlefish bone is obtainable in bird stores and a piece of it should always be kept inside the cage. It supplies the calcium necessary to a bird's diet. If this bone cannot be purchased, a piece of old mortar may be substituted. This may be picked up any place where a building is being torn down, and after being washed may be put on the cage floor or in the playpen. Occasionally a grain of table salt in the water is of benefit. Too much is dangerous.

Treat Foods

There are different kinds of ground foods offered in pet shops. Where the label analysis says the product contains cod-liver oil or vitamins A and D, only one-quarter teaspoonful of cod-liver oil is used per pound of seeds. Treat foods sold for parrakeets or budgerigars may be fed in a little treat cup. These foods should be fresh. It is wise to watch the bird's droppings. If diarrhea develops and the bird shows signs of not feeling well, the treat food may either be spoiled or contain ingredients which are indigestible for a budgerigar.

Some treat foods, also called conditioning food, are very good and greatly enjoyed by the birds. The proteins, vitamins, and minerals they contain will improve the bird's well-being and add to the luster of its coat of feathers. It is important that such foods not be old and rancid. Another kind of treat much relished by a budgie is spray millet. This type of millet is not threshed; the seeds are still on the head, and budgies delight in climbing the sprays, shelling and eating the seeds.

"Nibbles"

Allowing a bird to nibble from the dishes on the dinner table may be very cute but should not be tolerated. It is not hygienic

The slogan of a cattle breeder might well be adopted by breeders and keepers of better parrakeets: "Breed, feed, weed!" Supply your birds with supplementary nutritional elements otherwise lacking in the basic diet.

and may injure the bird's health. Birds are adapted to digest their regular diet and any new addition in the form of food meant for humans may result in constipation, bad feather growth, deficiency diseases, abnormal droppings, and general malaise. Many budgies are, therefore, locked up in their cages at mealtime and partake of their own food while the family is eating. This is a happy solution to the problem of how to keep the little pet out of mischief and at the same time keep him in good health.

Pet budgerigars make a beautiful display in the home. Budgies are more popular than canaries now.

Budgerigars are very romantic and attentive to each other. This pair is feeding each other prior to mating.

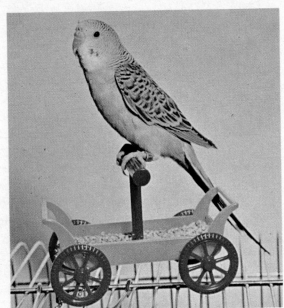

This "chow wagon" is one of the many toys available for your Budgie's entertainment. If you place it on a level table, your budgie might push it off onto the floor.

IV Care of the Baby Budgerigar

A baby budgie, newly arrived in his future home, demands special care. The needs of such a young bird, purchased from a breeder who specializes in preparing a budgerigar for talking, are numerous. On arrival the baby bird will be about six weeks old. Usually he has been tamed and his wing feathers have been clipped so that he cannot fly too high or too fast and injure himself. If he should bump against an uncovered window or a mirror, he will not suffer, but will soon learn to stop just before hitting these deceptive surfaces. A young bird with unclipped wing feathers often has no chance to learn by experience because the first encounter in full flight with a mirror might break his neck and thus end his life.

Food

If you have purchased a baby bird, your first duty is to see to it that he eats properly. A strange cage, a strange room, and a different way of handling may prove quite upsetting to the young budgie. As described in Chapter three, a shallow dish with the seed mixture treated with cod-liver oil should be kept on the cage floor until the bird knows where to find the seed cup. Birds eat practically all day long, but they take their main meal toward evening. At this time they fill their crops for the night. If a baby bird has not eaten during the first day, the perches may be taken out of the cage toward evening so that the bird will be forced to sit in the seeds on the floor. If left alone at this time, he will usually eat; if not, he will probably make up for it during the night or the following day. There is no cause to worry if the bird is about six weeks old and has been properly prepared for. Well washed greens will take the place of water should the bird fail to find the water cup. If you see your budgie eating, do not disturb him. Let him eat his fill without interruption.

Handling

The young budgerigar which has been tamed before sale never-theless requires handling several times a day so that he will not forget his tameness and become wild again. In general, it is safe to say that he cannot be handled too much, but where there are children in the house there is a danger that the young bird will never be left to himself. He is likely to be weakened by too fre-quent attention and may be denied a chance to eat enough. Under such conditions a bird may become irritable and peck at the handler. A child should not be allowed to take hold of a bird from above. He is likely to close his hand too tightly over the bird and squeeze it. It is best to allow a child to hold the bird on his finger only or to carry it on his shoulder. A grown person may close his hand around the bird from above and lift him up slowly while loosening the bird's feet gently from the perch with one finger.

Some baby budgies are afraid of a hand in the cage and prefer to be taken out on a stick or perch gently pressed against the breast. Allow him to fly a little around the room and do not worry if he hits the wall and drops to the floor. The clipped wing feathers make his flying awkward at first, but soon he will learn to know the room and will be able to control his flight better. If he should drop behind furniture, a T-stick (see Chapter six) will be helpful to rescue him. Put your forefinger against the bird's breast and he will step off the T-stick and on to your finger. Next put the fore-finger of the other hand against his breast and he will climb on it. This procedure may be continued, forefinger above forefinger, un-til the bird walks as on a ladder.

It is desirable that the budgie should get some flying exercise. He will soon learn to fly back to his cage, which means home and safety to him. It will take the young bird a while to find the door, but he will try again and again and finally succeed. To make it easier for him to find the entrance to the cage, a perch with a metal clasp may be fastened to the cage from the outside. This will give him a foothold next to the open cage door. If a baby bird perches somewhere in the room and stays there without moving, it is not wise to leave him there for long. He has not sense enough to return to his cage and food of his own accord, and there are no parent budgies to show him the way. He should be placed in the

Train your budgies to perch on your hand or finger and not on your head, as they so frequently do.

Sometimes called "Lovebirds," budgerigars often sit close together and "nuzzle."

If you band birds when they are three or four days old, you will have less difficulty slipping the bands on.

cage again or, better still, held on the finger a little distance from the cage to encourage him to fly to the door.

Quietness

Most baby birds are very quiet at first. This often worries the inexperienced owner. It is not unusual for the baby budgie to sit motionless for hours. Sometimes he begs to be let out of the cage, then flies to a perching place in the room and remains there, not taking advantage of his liberty. The birds vary greatly in behavior. Some are quieter than others. These individual differences have often caused the owner of a very quiet bird to worry after he has seen a much livelier young budgie in a friend's house. The quiet budgie usually is as healthy as the more active one and may make up later for his initial inactivity. One reason for excessive quietness may be lack of entertainment. Budgerigars in a group are active a great deal of the time. If the old birds fly around, the babies follow suit. If a baby sits in a listless manner, one of the parents may come around and give the youngster a punch on the head or back apparently to remind him that there is food to be searched for and that there are wings to be exercised. But a little budgie kept by himself cannot follow the example of his elders. He may not attempt to move unless he is taken out of his cage and given some attention by his owner.

Another reason for excessive quietness of the baby bird may be lack of sleep. His cage should be covered not later than seven o'clock at night. A bird kept in a well lighted room with the radio going and a number of people about until late every night does not get the proper rest, especially if his cage is covered with an almost transparent cloth. If possible, put the baby bird in a dark and quiet room or closet at sun-down and put him back into the living room after everyone has gone to bed. A bird kept up too late will be sleepy all day and will not eat properly. When he is older, he may gradually be allowed to stay up longer. Some budgies, while still babies, get attached to their owners. Such birds frequently do not want to go to bed, but want to stay in the room with people. Birds of this temperament have to be watched so they will get enough

A beautifully delicate Rainbow-budgie—impossible to differentiate between the subtle shades.

It is up to you to decide what color you want and what age bird you want. A young bird is a must if you want to train him. Older birds are for breeding purposes.

Parrakeets are good pets for children. This little girl is selecting a tame one at a pet shop.

sleep. A third reason for lack of liveliness may be that the bird has been exposed to a draft and is, therefore, not feeling well. If this cause is eliminated, there is nothing to worry about. It should be remembered that baby birds tend to be quieter than adult birds and must be entertained a great deal by their owners or they will not develop into good pets.

Attachment to Owner

Most budgerigars do not voluntarily fly to their masters until they are three or four months old. As a general rule it may be said that the more a baby bird has been played with the sooner will he become attached to his owner. However, some budgies are bold from the beginning. Others are reserved by nature and it will take longer to break the ice. Provided a young budgerigar receives a reasonable amount of attention, he will, after a relatively short time, make a charming pet and companion. It will give any bird lover a great thrill indeed when his young budgie makes the first clumsy attempts to fly to him and show signs of affection.

Taming

If an untamed young budgerigar has been purchased, the first step in taming him consists in clipping some of his long wing feathers. It is not advisable to leave a young budgerigar confined to his cage. He needs flying exercise and should be let out frequently, but a bird with unclipped wing feathers will fly around under the ceiling and insist on perching in high places. When an

Often a bird that sits docilely on your hand at the end of a lesson has become quite wild by the time you begin your next lesson. Ignore your budgie's wildness and your pet will soon calm down.

Budgie with overgrown upper beak.

A budgerigar with a splinted leg covered with plaster of Paris and tape. Leg fractures are common among psittacine birds kept in cages having wire floors of the improper mesh size.

attempt is made to put him back into his cage, he is likely to escape and must be caught. Chasing the bird around the room will frighten him and make him wild instead of tame. Clipped wing feathers, however, will slow down the speed of flying and prevent the bird from flying too high. He will be less confident of his flying ability and consequently will allow a person to approach him and will more readily step on a finger.

To clip the wing feathers, take the bird gently into your left hand, open one wing and cut off half the length of the long flight feathers (the so-called primaries) with a pair of sharp scissors, leaving the two longest ones on the outer edge untouched. Do the same with the other wing. If the bird can still fly too well, the pro-

CUT OFF

To slow down your budgie, but without preventing him from flying, clip the wing feathers. Cut all primaries except the outer two on both wings to half their length with a pair of sharp scissors.

Clipping feathers is neither cruel nor painful to the bird ... the feathers grow back, and it might save his life if he escapes!

cedure may be repeated by clipping some additional feathers on each wing (the so-called secondary flight feathers). If the bird is very wild he will bite the fingers that hold him, so it is advisable to wear gloves. Clipping the wing feathers should be done before any attempts at taming are made. Wing feathers should never be cut so severely that the bird cannot fly at all. He should be able to fly on an even keel.

Young children are as adept at teaching budgies to talk as are older people, but they should speak slowly and clearly so the bird will understand them and be better able to mimic them. Whether young or old, the teacher will have an easier time with a wing-clipped bird.

Some breeders or dealers pluck several wing feathers instead of clipping them. We do not advise any pulling of feathers because it is painful to the bird and often causes bleeding. The lower part of the quills of young feathers in young birds is filled with blood and should be left in place. The stumps will eventually dry up and fall out on their own accord. New feathers will grow and the bird will then be able to fly swiftly. In most cases the flight feathers are not clipped again because by the time their second growth is completed, the bird is tame and will remain where people are and not perch in high places. He will also have learned about mirrors and windows and not fly against them.

Sometimes all wing feathers are pulled or cut. Such a bird looks unnatural and crippled. Leaving the two outer feathers on each wing gives the bird a normal appearance and sufficient flying ability. No wounds are inflicted and the bird does not fall to the floor like a stone thus injuring his breast bone.

Some dealers and breeders do not believe in any cutting of wing feathers and advise keeping the bird in his cage for one to two weeks and tame him during that time. When let out after this initial training period, the bird is tame. There are various ways of

A quartet of budgerigars illustrating various color phases. At the far left is a Normal Sky; next to the blue are three birds that fall into the green category, indicating the change in color shade when the gray factor is added and when the sex-linked Cinnamon factor affects the basic color.

As the budgie becomes more and more tame, he will become more attached to his friend and trainer, and the reward will then be the trainer's mere presence. And what is nicer than being close together, almost face to face!

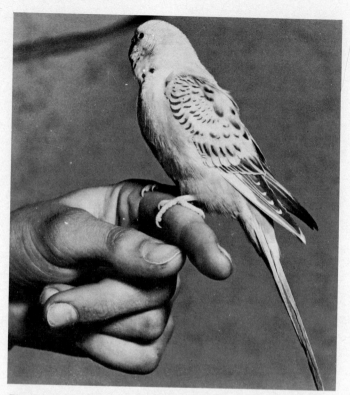

Finger training is simple and worthwhile when there is confidence between the bird and the trainer. Hold your finger very still and keep talking all the time.

handling a baby bird and different methods have led to success if the owner is kind and loving to the little pupil.

In taming the young budgerigar it is advisable to leave him in his cage and then push a stick through the bars until he ceases to be afraid of it. He will then step on the stick if pushed against his breast. Next, reach in slowly with your hand and let the bird get acquainted with it. After a while a finger may be pushed against the bird's breast; gradually he will learn to step on it. Taming a bird takes time and patience. Never frighten him and always approach him slowly. A tamed bird will seldom remain tame if he is put into a large cage with other birds or if he is never played with. A lone budgerigar can be kept tame much easier than two or more kept together.

Biting

If a budgerigar is teased too much, he may become a biter. All birds of the parrot family have strong beaks and will use them on their masters if annoyed. As a rule, a tame budgie, treated gently, does not bite. However, occasionally a tame young budgie may bite if pushed away from where he wants to be or if handled too roughly. Biting, too, may become a defense mechanism when the budgie is thwarted in his desires. If he is treated with understanding, he will soon forget about biting. Occasionally a young budgie will go through a biting phase apparently out of pure mischief. It is important to ignore such behavior and the budgie will outgrow this phase in most cases. Punishing a bird will only make matters worse. A bird kept up too late at night and played with incessantly may become very nervous and bite.

A single tame budgie, although he will seldom touch apple in his cage, will soon nibble on it when he sees his master eat one.

Both budgies are show quality birds with large heads and nice coloring. Color, however, has nothing to do with the ability to talk or to be tamed.

Hand-feeding of baby birds should be avoided if possible. It used to be thought that a young bird would not become entirely tame if not taken out of the nest at a very early age and hand-fed by the owner. This theory seems to have no foundation in fact. All that is necessary is to handle the birds in the nest as often as possible but to leave their feeding to the parent birds. A tame bird, however, likes to nibble on fruit, canary seed (because it is easier to crack) and such, offered in the hand.

Hand-feeding

A well-bred bird does not require hand-feeding at the age of five or six weeks. If he should not eat much the first day, there is nothing to worry about. If he does not eat after the second day, hand-feeding must be resorted to. Crush some seeds with a rolling pin just to crack the hulls, but do not make flour out of the seeds. Put the crushed seeds into a flat dish, take the bird into your left hand and push his beak into the seeds. It will take some time before the bird will start eating. Be patient and try it again and again. Or soak seeds over-night in water, drain, and urge the bird to eat. If the bird keeps on refusing, cook a mush of a mixture of oatmeal or cream of wheat with hard-boiled egg and bread crumbs. This must be fed warm. Have it fairly dry and fill a teaspoon with it. Hook the bird's beak over the edge of the teaspoon. Gradually he will start eating. If the mush cools, warm it up again in case the bird refuses to eat cold food. If this method does not work, try force-feeding the bird. Purchase a plastic tube with a plunger especially made for feeding birds and fill the tube with farina (baby food) moistened with warm milk. Force the tip of the tube into the bird's beak and press the food down his throat by means of the plunger. If some of the food escapes through the sides of the beak, the tube has not been pushed down far enough. One or two such feedings are usually sufficient to give the bird enough strength to eat from a teaspoon or to crack soaked seeds.

All hand-feeding should be done every two or three hours until the bird has gained strength and is eating well. Then the intervals may be lengthened. Any moist food adhering to some of the feathers must be removed with a small damp sponge or a soft cloth. The feathers must then be wiped dry so that the bird will not catch cold as a result of being wet or having his feathers stick together. During the period of hand-feeding, plenty of canary seeds and hulled or steel-cut oats should be kept on the bottom of the cage.

Twice a week, offer your budgie a seed bell or hang one in the cage, but do not consider it as part of the pet's basic diet; it is more of a treat and can be used as a reward when training the bird. Your pet store has a wide variety of seed bells for sale.

A fine painting by R.A. Vowles of a wild budgerigar. As can be seen, wild budgies are comparatively less stocky in build than our birds. Our domesticated birds are much bigger (up to 8½ inches, as opposed to about 7 inches for wild budgies) and heavier. Their basic diet is formed by canary seed and millet.

The African Gray Parrot (*Psittacus erithacus*), from central Africa, is the best known pet parrot in Europe and America and probably the best talker of all the parrots. African Grays have been bred on several occasions and are usually good parents.

Beautiful cages fitted with a gymnasium are available at your pet-shop. Consider the cage from a practical viewpoint. Your pet dealer will help you to make a sensible selection.

Below:
If through an accident to one or both parents the young cannot be transferred to other nests, hand-feeding becomes necessary; it should always be done with warm food.

V How to Teach the Budgerigar to Talk

It is not until after the advice given in the previous chapter on the care of a newly purchased baby budgerigar has been carefully followed during the first days, that the owner should start with talking lessons. It is most essential that the bird should be tame. This is the first requirement because an untamed bird will rarely learn to talk. The potential talker also must be kept out of sight and hearing of all other birds. If he hears a canary singing in the same room, he will copy his song and no human words. Any bird voice is easier for him to imitate than the human voice. Hearing a few sparrows or other birds call from outdoors does not seem to interfere with the budgie's learning to talk. He hears the wild birds only occasionally and even if he does answer them at first by chirping, he will soon forget about them.

A woman makes a better tutor than a man because she has a higher voice. A man, of course, can teach a bird to talk, but it is desirable that he try to pitch his voice a little higher. A budgerigar trying to imitate a low-pitched voice is likely to talk hoarsely and not clearly.

The first talking lesson consists of placing the bird on your finger and repeating one or two words over and over again in a loud and distinct voice. Do not say more than two words at first. It takes the young budgie two or three months to learn them. If more words are said, the bird will be confused and will take a much longer time to learn them.

Speak loudly because all birds belonging to the parrot family like noise and pay more attention to a loud voice than to a soft, low one. Moreover, the bird tries to imitate not only what you say, but how you say it. He is small in size and has only a small talking voice. If his lessons are given in a low voice, he will repeat in a low voice and may be hard to understand. If his lessons are given in a loud voice, he will speak louder and can be understood much better.

Budgies are obtainable in many different color varieties. Color has no influence on intelligence, adaptability or hardiness, nor does it determine the budgie's potential as a tame and talking pet. It is very important always to select a pet store in which the birds are healthy and happy looking.

The above cage is not suitable for your budgie. Your local pet store has better ones, like the one below. A good cage is approximately 9 inches deep, 18 inches wide and about 13 inches high; such a cage is suitable for a single budgie. Too small a cage results in a ragged set of tail feathers and a dirty looking bird. The bars should be set firmly and not wider apart than 1/2 inch with a 3/8 inch spacing preferred. There are a number of good cages at your pet shop made especially for budgerigars. They have horizontal bars (a budgie's bill is his third "foot") so he can climb to his heart's content. Natural tree branches with the bark left on make excellent perches; ready-made wooden perches are all right too, but plastic ones like the perches shown above are much less suitable. Our budgies deserve better.

When a budgie sits before a toy like a parakeet statue, talking to himself in his so-called bird language, it often seems as if he were talking human language very rapidly, with no clearly pronounced words but definitely with the same intonations.

The human voice may be amplified by speaking through a tube or tin can. "Pal" has learned many sentences in such a way from his teacher, who uses an empty can from which the top and bottom have been removed. The ends must be smooth and not ragged since Pal comes running across the playstand when a lesson begins and holds his head in the can. For better effect two such cans may be joined. This method helps greatly in training a bird to be a clear talker.

Speak slowly. It is characteristic of the budgerigar to speed up the words he is learning. If you speak fast, he will speak faster. Listen to his own little bird talk. He naturally talks very fast, saying many more syllables of his own invention than a person does during the same period of time. The best talkers are those who have been taught to speak slowly.

Young birds have a fully striped forehead, while older birds lose these baby stripes. The younger the bird and the oftener he receives talking lessons, the sooner will he learn to talk. Budgies kept in groups do not "mimic".

Speak distinctly. In speaking slowly, one usually does speak distinctly, but special emphasis should be given to each syllable. One bird, which was taught in a loud and slow voice to say "Bobby is just precious," insisted on saying, "Bobby is just presh." The last syllable had not been pronounced clearly enough and the bird left it out. It took an extra two weeks to make the young pupil say it correctly. And don't mumble baby talk to a budgerigar during lessons!

Lessons should be given as often as possible. The younger the bird and the oftener he receives talking lessons, the sooner will he learn to talk. Shut out all other noises, hold the bird on your finger and teach him systematically. Do this several times during the

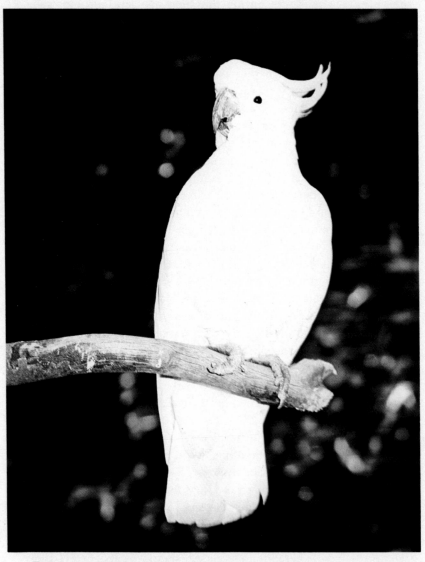

Truly experienced bird fanciers often graduate into becoming keepers of the more expensive and difficult to maintain parrot species after they've obtained sufficient experience with birds like budgies and Cockatiels. The Cockatoo shown here is the Greater Sulphur-crested Cockatoo, *Cacatua galerita*.

A young male Cockatiel approximately eight months of age. This bird makes a fine pet.

morning, several times during the afternoon and evening, and once when the bird is in his cage and covered up for the night. The lesson in the dark is usually quite effective. The bird cannot see anything to distract him and will listen more intently. At other times of the day when you pass him in his cage or on his playground, repeat the words he is to learn. Do not say anything else to him but these words. Always use the same intonation because different intonations of the same words will sound like different words to the bird and this may retard learning. The first word usually taught a bird is his name. The average age at which he will have learned to repeat it is four months. Some bugerigars learn to talk sooner, some later. The method used in teaching and handling the bird has much to do with the speed at which he will learn. It was thought that a budgerigar could not learn to talk under the age of three months; however, this theory has been disproved. One baby budgie, at the age of two and a half months, after only one month in his new home, surprised everyone with the words, "Sweet little birdie, my little blue bird." The bird said the whole phrase frequently and distinctly at this early age. The bird belonged to an invalid lady, eighty years old, who sat all day in her chair near the window and who occupied herself by repeating these words innumerable times. The little budgie soon became attached to the old lady and these two became pals. The bird did not show any affection for the other members of the family. Latest records show that quite a number of budgies have started to talk at two months of age.

Next to tameness, affection for the tutor is an important factor. The more a bird is handled and played with, the sooner will he become attached to his owner and the sooner will he learn to talk, provided he is receiving regular lessons. If too many different persons try to teach him, the young budgie may become confused. If there are many adults and children in the house, all are likely to talk to the bird. Therefore, one person should be assigned to the task of giving systematic lessons during times when it is quiet.

A newly purchased baby budgie does not say much, not even in his own language. He chirps occasionally, but usually does not start with his own bird talk until he has been in his new home for a while. However, he will have talked his own "language" for some time before he begins to imitate our language. The first real word

Other bird species will not sit upon a stranger's finger without considerable training, but a budgie's behavior codes include no offishness or stiffness. They're usually glad to come to hand.

uttered by a little budgerigar after many weeks of patient teaching gives a great thrill to the owner. The bird will not say it perfectly at first, nor very often, but soon all efforts will be rewarded and the young budgie will delight his tutor in saying his name many times a day. When he repeats his name perfectly, he should be taught a short phrase such as, "Want a kiss?" with two kissing sounds after it. With systematic teaching, the bird will have mastered such a phrase in about two weeks. If necessary, allow another week for the perfect mastery of the phrase; then proceed to teach him another short phrase such as "Let's have a party" or "Let's play the piano."

The first real word uttered by a little budgie after many weeks of patient teaching gives a great thrill to the owner. The bird will not say it perfectly at first, nor very often, but soon all efforts will be rewarded and the young budgie will delight his tutor in saying his name many times a day. By the way, a budgie sitting on it's owner's shoulder nibbles on everything within reach: clothing, jewelry and . . . flesh. A mirror does keep a budgie fascinated, but if there is a way of getting into trouble, the budgie is sure to find it.

After the young budgerigar has learned several phrases, a longer sentence may be taught. It will be found that the more he learns, the quicker he masters new words. In teaching a sentence, always say the whole sentence through from beginning to end. If the bird does not repeat certain parts properly, do not correct those parts alone, but say the whole sentence again and again, emphasizing the syllables that have not been properly pronounced by the little pupil. Needless to say, the longer the sentence, the more time will be required by the bird to repeat it correctly. This is the reason why the budgerigar should only be taught short phrases at first while he is still learning slowly. A bird with a vocabulary of fifteen to twenty-five words will pick up others very fast. Sometimes only a couple of days are needed for an accomplished talker to learn a new phrase. One two-year-old budgie with a vocabulary of one hundred words repeated a phrase during the afternoon of the same day it had been said to him for the first time. Lengthy sentences and complicated nursery rhymes, of course, will always take longer periods of teaching.

There are some sounds a baby budgerigar does not like to repeat. M, n, and l are letters which should be used only sparingly when a baby is receiving his first talking lessons. Words starting with p, t, or k are quickly learned and therefore the baby's first words should be something like "Pretty bird," or "Pretty boy." Some young birds have difficulty pronouncing the letter s properly. Emphasis on words starting with an s will overcome this defect in diction. Among all the many birds we have trained we had only one who refused to say s. We selected words containing an s and actually hissed them at the poor little pupil while he was still under one year of age. The method was crowned with success. During his long life he learned innumerable words containing an s and pronounced them perfectly. An adult talker, with patient tutoring, will learn to say any letter of the alphabet. One budgerigar called Jacky, was taught to say, "Ladies and Gentlemen, how do you do?" He insisted on saying, "Ladies and Jacky," etc. The owner persisted, but it took a whole summer of continual teaching to make the bird say "gentlemen."

The quality of a budgerigar's talking voice varies considerably. Some birds talk very clearly, while others do not. This is due partly to differences in the birds themselves and partly to the methods of teaching. A bird from a strain of clear-voiced talkers is likely to have a better talking voice than one from an unknown strain or one that has produced hoarse talkers. However, a great deal always depends upon the way in which the bird is taught. One very distinct talker was sold and in a few months his exceptionally clear voice had degenerated into a weak, mumbly one. The new owner merely kept up the bird's vocabulary by occasional repetition, but did not use as clear or as loud a voice as the first trainer. This shows that a clear talker can be spoiled by wrong teaching methods. To be sure, some birds will never be able to talk clearly, no matter how carefully trained, as is the case with canaries. A common canary will not be able to repeat the song of a fine roller canary, no matter how many opportunities he may be given to learn the roller song. A fine roller, on the other hand, will soon lose the perfection of his song if he does not hear anything but common canaries.

A young budgie placed with a good talker may learn to talk by imitation.

A budgerigar learns to repeat human language best if he is tame and attached to a person. Mechanical sounds usually are not repeated. One talking budgie kept in a room where a cuckoo clock struck every half hour never repeated the cuckoo sound. As far as is known, the sound of door and telephone bells have not been repeated by talking budgies. However, laughing, sneezing, coughing, and clearing the throat have been imitated readily. The tinkling of the bells on the playstand or in the cage is frequently repeated. These bells are punched by the budgie and, therefore, play an important role in his life. Dog barking has not been imitated, but the chirping of other birds has been repeated. The rhythm of conversation among people is often well reproduced. When the bird sits before his mirror, talking to himself in his so-called bird language, it often seems as if he were talking human language very rapidly, with no clearly pronounced words, but definitely with the same intonations. A group of budgerigars kept together do not produce bird talk of this kind. They keep up a warbling song, quite different from the bird talk of a lone budgie that lives with human beings.

In teaching a bird to count, it will help to use rhythm. A budgerigar does not seem to care much for one, two, three, four, five, six. . . said in a monotone, but he does respond if the voice is, for instance, raised at three and dropped at six.

Whistling Melodies

It is not hard to teach a budgerigar to whistle a melody. Use the same methods as described for teaching to talk—whistling only a few bars to the bird at first. When he has mastered these, whistle a melody. It is best that the bird should learn to talk before he is trained to whistle because whistling is easier to learn. A whistling bird often will not want to learn to talk. Some female budgies that are slow in learning to talk have developed into outstanding whistlers.

Teaching to Sing

To sing words is always hard for a budgerigar. He has not a wide range of voice and cannot repeat the low tones. A simple melody should be chosen and it should be sung to him in a fairly

A budgie's voice is small, and the bird has a tendency to speak faster than we do and run the words together. Therefore it is important during training that you speak more slowly than you would normally, enunciating each word clearly and pausing for a few moments at the end of each word.

high voice, only one or two bars at a time. When the bird has mastered these, proceed to add a few more bars. It will take many months for the budgie to learn to sing a song and it will take much patient tutoring by the owner. But a talking and singing budgerigar is priceless, and the efforts to teach him are repaid many times by the fame such a bird may bring to his master.

The Non-talking Budgerigar

The most common reason for the failure to learn to talk is that the bird has not been isolated early enough from his parents and all other birds. Other reasons are that he has not been taught systematically, that too many different people have tried to teach him, or that the owner has become discouraged too soon and has stopped saying the same one or two words over and over again. A budgerigar left alone too much of the time may lose interest in his owner and in the talking lessons. He may be tame, step readily on a finger, but will not voluntarily fly to a person. Such a neglected little budgie will not learn to talk unless a special effort is made by the owner to overcome the bird's independence, acquired by being left alone too much. It will take a much longer time to teach a bird like this to talk because habits already established have to be broken first before the bird will even listen to his tutor. Nevertheless, it is possible to teach a budgerigar to talk even after he has reached the age of six months. But by far the easiest way to teach a budgie to talk is to spend much time with him during the first few months. The bird will become attached to his owner and then readily repeat the owner's language. "A stitch in time saves nine." We doubt whether any budgie can resist learning to talk if he receives a talking lesson for five minutes out of every hour.

It is possible that your budgie turned out to be a female. If the cere (the waxy skin around the nostrils) shows a whitish tan instead of a rich blue color at the age of six months, the bird is a little hen instead of a cock. Some hens do not want to talk, but many female budgies have learned to talk though it may take a little longer to teach them. An Opaline hen we know of can out-talk any male. There are many females now that are good talkers. The most important factor in training is not to give up talking lessons when it becomes apparent that the bird is a female. Female budgies will learn to whistle exceedingly well and many have learned to talk from a male talking bird.

Moreover, female birds often make superior trick birds since they are less excitable than males. It should be mentioned in this connection that the basal metabolic rate of the female has been found to be lower than that of the male. A lone female is a charming pet and as amusing as a male. Many an owner of a female non-talking budgie would not part with her for a thousand dollars. A considerable number of people have told us they prefer females as pets—be it dogs, cats, or birds.

The Talking Budgerigar as a Teacher

In some instances a female budgie has learned to talk by being kept in the same room with a male talking budgerigar. She will sometimes learn to imitate the talker though she will not imitate the words of a person. Available reports indicate that in many cases the speech of the talker suffers from hearing the chatter of the female. A bird learning from another bird often repeats words incorrectly or incompletely. There is no way of correcting a bird, male or female, which has learned to imitate another bird since it will as a rule not listen to the words from a person. It is not advisable to keep two budgerigars, one or both of which are talkers, in a room together for any length of time. They tend to become very excited by the sight of another bird of their kind; they tend to prefer the company of the other budgerigar to that of their master and will bite when an attempt is made to separate them. Two budgies often stimulate each other to screech and thus become too noisy. A lone budgie rarely screeches. If he does, he may only be passing through a phase which he will get over because he hears no answering screeches. Teaching him more phrases is likely to take his mind off the screeching.

The above is the experience of many budgie owners. However, these birds are not all alike—each has a different personality. Many people have kept two budgies in the same room (although not the same cage) and both have been talkers. Frequently the first budgie is tamed and taught to talk before a second, younger bird is introduced; the older bird then teaches the baby to become tame and to talk. It is important, however, to give the first bird thorough training before adding the second one.

Budgerigar breeders often keep a tame and talking older pet bird to teach the babies how to be nice pets. A baby bird is very imitative and when seeing the older bird perching fearlessly on a human hand, it will do the same. Many people are not as interested in talkers as they are in tame pets which play with toys and with each other. Birds which receive a great deal of human attention often try to compete with each other when their mistress (or master) enters the room. They are lovable pets and at the same time talk enough to satisfy the owner.

There are not many perfect talkers in the country. We refer here to birds with a vocabulary of several hundred words, well pronounced and plainly spoken. Such superior birds are invariably kept alone with no other birds in the same room. Occasionally accounts and pictures of such outstanding specimens are found in the daily newspaper.

One trainer, experienced in the handling of budgerigars, has reported success in keeping two talking birds in the same house. She has allowed the birds to fly together for a few hours each day, but has otherwise kept them in different rooms. Each bird was tutored separately by the trainer and the occasional visits have neither interfered with the ability of the birds to learn additional words and sentences nor with their attachment to the owner. These visits, however, were not allowed before each bird had mastered a vocabulary of fifteen to twenty-five words.

Broadcasting and Television

Mr. Andrew Wilson, F.Z.S., reports from England that talking budgerigars have frequently performed in radio programs. Their little talking voices come over the air so clearly that it is hard for listeners to believe that it is actually a bird talking and not a person. Mr. Wilson points out that the recording has to be made in the house where the bird lives since a budgerigar will seldom talk in strange surroundings. The sentences which are reproduced perfectly in the recording are later transferred to another record, leaving out unwanted noises and incomplete sentences. Such a record may then be used in a radio program whenever desired. Of course, the bird selected for broadcasting must talk clearly and distinctly. He should also be a bird that says a sentence perfectly from beginning to end. Some birds occasionally mix up what they have learned, which may be confusing during a broadcast although otherwise amusing.

In this country tame budgerigars are seen more and more often in television programs. They have performed with or without their owners, have advertised coming cage bird exhibitions, bird supplies, etc. Pet budgies are very fond of watching television at home and are especially pleased when they recognize their own kind on the screen.

Making the Talker Talk

Sometimes a visitor comes from afar to hear a famous budgerigar talk. The owner does everything he can think of to induce his bird, usually an industrious talker, to say a few sentences. But the budgie will not talk. The visitor, after a long time of patient waiting, disappointedly leaves and soon after his departure the bird starts cheerfully to say a long nursery rhyme and whistle a melody. The failure of the budgie to perform when asked to is a sad and not uncommon experience to the proud owner of an outstanding bird and also to the visitor who was so anxious to hear a budgerigar talk.

What can be done to make a talker talk at a certain time? There are ways that sometimes bring results, but there is no sure method. One way is to let water run from a tap. The noise may stimulate the budgerigar to talk. Another method that has worked very well in some instances is to put the budgie in his cage and cover it with a dark cloth. After a short time the bird, probably bored with the darkness about him, may start and keep up his linguistic exercise for quite a while. Another talker would perch on some books, standing between bookends, and start talking there, addressing the tallest book. When placed on these books by the owner, this little scholar would five times out of six start to talk to his favorite book. Still another bird could always be started talking by the sound of rustling paper. A number of birds have the habit of talking only baby talk or their own bird language when looking into a mirror. When they are expected to say their sentences, the mirror must be covered. Soon after that, these birds may begin to talk. If a budgie likes to talk to a polished fingernail, or a shiny ring, put him near these attractive objects and often he can be induced to talk, especially if his beak is tapped lightly with the fingernail.

In brief, it is necessary to study the habits of each individual bird. Perhaps a method can be found to make the bird talk at a given time. The adopted method may not work every time, especially not at first, but its patient use may decrease the number of disappointments to an appreciable degree. If a person talks to a bird, the little pupil will listen intently and not say a word himself. He will remain silent as long as he is being addressed. It is important, therefore, to advise a visitor to ignore the bird that he wants to hear talk. To be sure, there are some exceptional birds which immediately respond to a known phrase. For instance, the bird is asked, "Will you talk to me?" and echoes, "Will you talk to me?"

Some birds may be trained to answer questions. For example, the little pupil is taught to reply, "Very well, thank you," to the question "How are you today?" Hearing the question may provide the bird with the cue for giving the answer.

Splitting the Tongue

It is not necessary to perform any kind of operation on a bird's tongue, as for instance cutting a tendon, to make him talk more clearly. This cruel practice is not justified in talking birds in general. The true vocal organ is the syrinx situated below the larynx and found in birds only. The tongue of a budgerigar is thick, rubbery and dry and plays only a slight role in formulating all the minute differences in tone and accent which are so faithfully reproduced by this bird. For this reason, an injury to his tongue cannot lead to any improvement of his talking and will only do harm.

Phonograph Teaching

Teaching a young budgie to talk by playing a record to him may be of help. It is best, however, to first teach him by mouth. Only in this way will the bird become used to copying his master and become attached to him or her. Later a record may be used to reinforce the talking lessons. The one great disadvantage of using a record is that the "s" does not sound clearly enough for the bird to copy it correctly. Consequently only words not containing an "s" should be played to the bird on a record.

Records especially designed to teach a bird to talk are offered on the market and may be ordered through your pet shop. In addition there are recording studios in most cities and a person can go there and have his or her own voice recorded. One chosen phrase is said over and over again until the record is filled. A different phrase is recorded on the other side of the disc. Training can also be accomplished through use of a tape recorder.

Bells and beads are fastened with strings, not wires. Note the plastic budgie and metal mirror on top. The bells at the right have been selected by tone. Candy strikes one bell in such a way that all the bells are set into motion, sounding a melody.

VI The Budgerigar as a Trick Bird

A tame single budgie, whether a talker or not, whether a male or female, enjoys inventing his own tricks. The first requirement to keep your budgie happy is to place in his cage one or more bells that he can ring and punch. Often he pushes his head under a bell of the open type with a clapper and sits there with the bell over his head like a helmet. Or he moves his head under the bell in such a way that the rim will scratch his head. Occasionally a bird will ring his bell in the morning to remind his master that he is awake and wants to have the cover taken off his cage and the door opened.

A playground affords a means of keeping a budgie happily occupied. The bird will fly over to it and spend much time there. It will keep him from selecting a perching place inconvenient for the owner or one near a drafty door or window. The illustrations show different types of playgrounds which provide the budgie with entertainment for years. He will hang upside down from a top perch, punching a bell, or will try to do the same by climbing up a vertical pole. He will sit for hours on the perch before a little mirror. He will admire himself and then jump to the floor of the playpen and pick up papers or short pieces of string. He will throw bottle caps about, push marbles, and chew on short pieces of wood. If he is playing on a table, he will endeavor to carry things to the edge and drop them overboard, peeking after them as they fall. On one occasion a man before leaving the house emptied the contents of his pockets on the sofa. There were match holders, crumpled cigarettes, two pencils, some coins, a pocket knife, calling cards, pieces of paper, etc. On his return at night, he found every one of these articles, including the heavy pocket knife, on the floor before the sofa. The budgie was asleep in his cage, the door of which was never closed.

Playstands provide endless fun. Various types are offered in pet shops and the budgie owner will derive a great deal of pleasure from selecting different toys for the playstand. Illustrated, for instance, is a farmyard with animals made of rubber. A playful budgie may pick up a horse by the heel and flip it into the air. Some greens, oats or a favorite toy may be used to coax the bird into the barn. In case of female budgies it is advisable not to make the barn too inviting. Since these birds breed in hollows, they may mistake the barn for a nest cavity and feel tempted to lay eggs.

Toys for budgies may be of different colors, as these birds see colors much the way we do. Some owners of tame budgerigars have observed that red is the least popular color for their pets. One owner reports that her bird definitely prefers yellow. The sense of play seems to be more highly developed in members of the parrot family than in other birds. You should, therefore, provide your budgie with toys. This should be done while the bird is young, because a mature budgie may not show interest in a playground or toys he has never seen before.

A Ping-pong ball hung up on a string at the right height for the bird to push it with his beak will serve as an ideal punching bag. Take care that the budgie cannot become entangled in the string. A set of Tinker-Toys provides endless fun.

In addition to the tricks a budgerigar invents himself, there are some that can be taught. Only a few simple tricks will be mentioned here.

Swinging on the T-Stick

Take a wooden stick three or four feet long and attach a little cross stick about four or six inches long to one end. This device will look like a T with a long handle and is incidentally very convenient to use when a bird perches in high places and will not come down when called. Push the T-stick against his breast so that he will be forced to step on it or else be pushed over backwards. When you have him on the T-stick, move the bird in a vertical circle, slowly at first. Begin the motion at the top of the circle and move downward in the direction of the bird's tail. In this way the bird is moved backwards and he will step forward in order to keep his balance on the turning perch. If he flies off, he should be put right back again. Soon the budgie will learn to stay on the stick and keep his balance whichever way he is moved—whether he is swayed like a pendulum or is moved in a horizontal or vertical circle.

Running Up a Ladder

A budgie will quickly learn to go up a ladder with rungs one and one-half inches apart. Push him a little at first and do not allow him to fly away or go up half the ladder only. He should go up the whole length without slipping away through the space between rungs.

Climbing a Rope

A window cord is best as it is thick enough for the bird to get a good hold. Make a loop at one end and slip it over your foot. Have the other end in your hand and hold the rope taut. After the budgie once gets the idea what you want him to do, he will do it. Just be patient. Put him at the foot end of the rope and push him up. Do this over and over again. Finally he will understand and busily climb up as soon as he is put on the floor near the rope.

Walking a Tight Rope

Do the same as above with a rope fastened tightly in a horizontal position. He will soon learn how to walk across the rope.

Skinning the Cat

This is a trick a young budgie may teach himself if confined to a cage. He will hook his feet into the wires and push his head through his legs, so that his feet are over his back. It is hard to understand how he will get himself disentangled again, but he always does.

Opening a Match Box

By means of adhesive tape attach a match box to a table so that the box will remain in position when the bird tries to open it. Put some oats or greens inside and leave the box open just a crack, so that the bird can see what is inside. Soon he will take hold of the drawer and pull it open.

Jumping

Suspend a small hoop made of wood or cardboard a little above a table and urge the bird to jump through. At first he will need a little pushing from behind. After a while the hoop can be suspended a little higher.

A bird can also be taught to jump over a pencil held above the table at various distances. One budgie always insisted upon jumping over the pencil in one direction. He would not turn and jump back, but would walk all the way around and then jump as before.

Riding a Car

Place the bird on a small toy car which has been equipped with a little perch and pull the car around the room. If the bird flies off, put him right back again. A mechanical car or electric train may also be used. A grandmother and her small grandson invented a charming game. One sat at each end of a long hallway; their budgie rode on an electric automobile which ran back and forth between them. All three enjoyed the game immensely.

Walking Through a Tunnel

Out of cardboard or wood build a tunnel wide enough for the bird to walk through but too narrow for him to turn back easily. Make the tunnel about one foot long at first. Place the bird in one end and hold your hand across the opening so that the bird cannot back out but must walk through to the other end. After he has learned that, the tunnel may be made longer. To provide adjustable lengths, round cardboard holders, such as those used for darning cotton, may be attached to each other. Then more can be added to make the tunnel longer if desired. One budgie loves to go into the middle of his tunnel and start talking, apparently enjoying his echo.

The Big Voice

Sometimes a budgie will stick his head into an outside seed cup and talk to hear his voice amplified. Or he will sit on the edge of a glass half-filled with water, lower his head, and listen to the reflection of sound from his voice. Then he will lower his head and talk into the glass—the big voice again. This cannot easily be taught; it

Jacky has a lot to say when he emerges from his tunnel.

is one of the tricks a clever budgie invents for his own amusement and that of the family.

"Dead Bird"

Most adult budgies, although tame, do not like to be enclosed by a hand. But a baby budgie does not object and this is the time to teach him to play dead. Take the bird into the hand, turn him over on his back and then slowly open the hand. A foot that may cling to a finger should be dislodged. Stroke his breast or head and say, "dead bird." Soon the budgie learns and lies motionless with his little feet in small fists above him.

Our own pet learned this trick after he was two years old. He likes to hang on the edge of the wooden frame of the bathroom mirror. While there, we stroked his wings and soon he let us take him into the hand to make him play dead. He does try to nibble at our fingers, so he is not a model "dead bird." Sometimes stroking a bird's head will hypnotize him and he will be a well-behaved "dead bird."

The Boomerang

Take the bird in your hand and then throw him (not too forcefully) down the length of a hallway or long room, and the budgie will turn in mid-air and fly back to you.

111

Flapping Wings

Clap your hands softly in front of the bird, at the same time lifting and lowering your elbows and saying: "Shall we fly?" After many repetitions the bird will imitate your motions and flap his wings. Later you do not need to move your arms any more. When "shall we fly?" is said, the bird will flap his wings.

Pulling Up Food in a Bucket

This trick is performed while the budgie is inside his cage which has a little porch attached to the upper level. The porch has an opening in the floor and is closed in on all other sides so the bird cannot escape. It contains a pulley with a jewelry chain running over it. The chain extends down through the opening in the floor of the porch and is attached to a little bucket filled with budgie's favorite food. Until the little pupil has understood what is expected of him, he is not allowed to eat anything for two hours before lessons. Then he is placed near the pulley and shown the food bucket below. He is coaxed to take hold of the chain with his beak and pull up the bucket, gripping the loops of the chain with his foot.

The porch with the pulley may be constructed at home by a mechanically minded person. It is attached to the side of the cage or hooked over the open door if there is one at the upper story of the cage. During the first lessons the bucket should be placed only a short distance below the opening; gradually the distance is increased while the bird learns to hold more loops of chain under his foot. It takes much time and much patience to perfect this trick, but a bird that has mastered it will be worth his weight in gold. Soon he will delight in pulling up seeds, greens, treat food, or water from a well and will enjoy hearing the little bucket bang against the cage wires when swinging while it is pulled up.

Teachers as well as birds vary in their abilities. Birds that do not learn to pull up the chain will sometimes bring it up successfully if the pulley is provided with a crank. The beak is hooked over the handle of the crank and the bird urged to turn it.

A simple modification of this trick is not hard for a budgie to learn. The pupil is placed in a cage fitted with outside cups. One cup is removed and a piece of wood or cardboard leads up to the opening from the outside. A little box is attached to a chain or

Pulling up food in a bucket is a difficult trick, but one worth teaching a trained budgie. A little perch should be attached to the side of the cage and a chain pulley fastened to permit a small bucket of food to be pulled through the bottom. The budgie is taught to pull the chain with his beak and hold the loops with a foot.

The punching bag at the right is attached to a spring; this is one of the most favored budgie toys.

string and the bird is taught to pull in the chain which will bring the box near enough so that the bird can reach it and eat the good things in it. The box may be on wheels and will roll back down the incline of the board unless the bird holds the string or chain with his foot. A light weight toy truck may be used.

Somersault

"Kiki" is an expert at this. His owner touched his bell which made Kiki run across the table in a hurry to defend it. His owner held a finger against the bird's legs to trip him. The budgie slipped, fell over and landed on his back. He liked it so well that he came back for more and this game is being played many times a day now.

Budgie on a Chain

There is a chain on the market designed to be attached to a budgie's foot. At times it is convenient to keep a bird from escaping by this means, but care should be taken that the bird receives proper training to wear the chain. A baby bird will be less upset by the chain than an older bird.

After the chain has been fastened on the bird's leg, it is best to place the bird on the floor and give him time to get used to it. The chain should not be held in a hand but should lie on the floor without being attached to an object. The budgie may roll about on the rug and bite his foot or the chain, but soon will tire of the struggle. Then the bird is picked up and the chain held loosely in the hand. As soon as the bird gets excited again, it is advisable to let go of the chain for a while. Birds with moderately clipped wing feathers are less likely to injure themselves while learning to fly with a chain on the foot.

A bird should always be under supervision while wearing a chain. After he has become used to it, he will be a better compa-

This playyard is attached to chains and suspended from a wall. Budgie's toys are placed on the wooden platform.

nion for an invalid who is unable to get up and retrieve a bird that has flown to another room or is hiding.

Caution must be exercised when taking a bird on a chain in the open. A well-trained bird will not get into trouble, but it has happened that a dog or cat has frightened a bird into flying up quickly causing him to sprain, or even break, a leg. Before taking a bird outdoors it is necessary to ascertain whether he can pull his foot through the ring and thus free himself of the chain.

Bringing Down a Flag

A perch of small diameter (about three-eighths of an inch) may be mounted on a base in an upright position. A flag is attached to a

There is no end to the amusement that a budgie can have on this log. No pine or other evergreens should be used. Logs from most leaf-bearing trees are safe.

wooden peg and this is fitted into a hole drilled into the top of the pole. When the budgie is placed near the pole and pushed a little, he will soon learn that he is expected to climb the pole, take the wooden peg on top into his beak and pull to dislodge it. To teach him this he is taken into the hand and his beak is hooked over the wooden peg. With patient training and much repetition the bird will soon learn.

A little cross bar on top for the bird to sit on will make it easier for him. Then he should slide or climb down the pole while carrying the flag in his beak. To keep the budgie from flying away while learning, a hand may be cupped over his head.

Fortune Telling

A budgie who has seen the family play cards will also become interested in card games. The person who wants his or her fortune told shuffles the cards and spreads them out on the table face down. The budgie is allowed to choose three cards which he will pull out from the others and, if he can be made to do so, flip over, face up. Little books are available in stores telling how fortunes are read from cards. Consulting one of these will soon make the budgie and his owner experts at fortune telling.

The Budgie Circus

A group of budgies can be taught to do tricks. For instance, the birds can be made to sit on a playground. While one or two are led through their paces, climbing ladders up and down, walking tight ropes, going through tunnels etc., the rest will wait their turn. Then all may ride on a toy train or merry-go-round.

As has been observed by trainers here and abroad, budgerigars make very adept pupils. They learn more and quicker than any of the brightest birds among the finches, including canaries. Two can be taught to sit at the ends of a teeter-totter, while a third one perches in the center and, on command, walks back and forth tilting the teeter-totter up and down. A budgie placed on his back on a table will learn to roll up a celluloid ball with his feet. The ball has to be provided with holes in which the bird can insert his toes while rolling the ball. Some will walk a tight rope carrying a parasol or balancing a rod in their beak. Others can be taught to drive an automobile, changing speeds by pulling a lever. A number of different tricks can be developed by utilizing the fact that the budgie will pull objects. He will also learn to perform on a trapeze or slide down a rope suspended diagonally, holding on with his beak only. One budgie may learn to shoot off a toy cannon while another is hoisting a flag.

There are many more tricks a group of circus budgies may be taught. The training takes unending patience, an understanding of what a bird is able to learn, and a great deal of time. It takes close to a year to teach a bird some of the more complicated tricks, especially those which involve obeying commands. The simpler tricks can be taught a young bird in a few days. The amateur budgie circus has often stolen the show at benefit performances and at parties.

The professional magician, too, has recognized the intelligence and adaptability of budgerigars and in many cases has trained them to co-operate in the most complicated disappearing and re-appearing acts. At a given signal the budgie flies from one cage into another behind a screen or runs up inside one sleeve and down another.

There is no end to the surprising stunts a young budgie will learn.

The tricksters in this chapter have been called "he," but this does not mean that male birds learn tricks easier. On the contrary, many trainers choose female birds because they often learn tricks better than males.

VII Health and Disease

Excellent books have been published on the ailments that afflict birds. The purpose of this chapter is mainly to suggest how to avoid disease and how to keep your little budgerigar healthy. A well bird is bright of eye and wears his feathers smooth and tight. A sick bird has a dull eye, sits around sadly and takes no interest in anything. If an indisposition is allowed to continue, he will soon look puffed up like a little ball, put his head under his feathers and even stop eating. A well bird draws up one foot when sleeping or resting; a sick bird sleeps with both feet on the perch. There is one exception to this: a very young baby bird in perfect health may sit during the day sleeping with his head tucked under his feathers and with both feet on the perch.

To keep your bird healthy you should, first of all, keep him out of drafts. Innumerable cage birds have died as a result of being kept too close to a window, even a double window. Locked up in their cages, they cannot escape the constant draft which may not be noticeable to a human being but may in time end a bird's life. When you notice your bird sneezing, try to discover how he might have caught cold. A cover over the cage at night helps to keep drafts away from him. In winter a bird may perch close to a drafty window, especially if this is his favorite spot. One bird did just that, became listless and one day collapsed on the floor and died. The autopsy showed congested lungs.

It is better to avoid sickness by learning how a bird should be kept than trying to cure him with drugs after his health has become impaired. Only simple remedies are given here because doctoring with tonics and bird bitters of unknown composition may hasten his end, while warmth and sensible care may give nature a chance to repair the damage. For puzzling and serious disorders a trained veterinarian should be consulted. A layman at times administers remedies for a disease which are not for the ailment from which the bird suffers; the real cause of the trouble thus remains untreated. Even a veterinarian cannot cure all ills, and it is best, therefore, to obtain a healthy bird and keep him in good condition.

Baths. A budgerigar does not take baths like a canary, though occasionally one has been seen to do something similar. He usually prefers being sprayed or, better still, having a little water thrown over him when you are washing your hands. See that this is not done in the afternoon. It takes feathers quite a while to dry thoroughly; spray him in the morning only. If a sneeze should develop, no more showers for about a week! It is better not to experiment with a baby bird in winter. Wait until the weather has become warm. Running water fascinates these birds, especially when their master has his hand in it. Then they want to get into the water also. On the Australian plains budgerigars take their baths by rolling in the dew wet grass. For that reason a budgie may be induced to take his bath in a bunch of wet carrot leaves. One bird went into raptures when a bunch of dew-laden pea vines was brought into the house. Another bird developed the habit of taking a bath every Sunday. When one was offered to him during the week, he refused it.

It is difficult to keep a pet budgie away from the kitchen sink when vegetables are being washed with a spray. Cold water is preferred by the budgie to tepid or warm water. Some of these birds bathe in ash trays or bird baths, roll over and become so wet they cannot fly. They must then be kept off the floor and away from drafts and cold.

Treatment of Colds. If a bird sneezes and coughs, sits quietly and closes his eyes, he should be confined to his cage. It is advisable to cover the cage on three sides during the day to exclude all possible draft but to admit enough light for the bird to see his food. When he is sick, he should be kept at a temperature of ninety degrees, his normal body temperature being one hundred and five degrees Fahrenheit. A hospital cage with thermostatically controlled head has been made available on the market. It is reasonable in price and may save the life of a precious budgie. After a day or so the bird usually picks up and is soon his old self again. If the cold is severe, he will breathe either heavily or quickly; he will sleep most of the time and stop eating. A bird loses strength rapidly if he cannot be coaxed to eat. Warm milk given with a medicine dropper may pull him through, the milk giving him sustenance during the time he cannot eat and digest seeds. Sometimes four or five drops of whiskey added to a tablespoon of milk has proved of

The terrifying size of this double tumor covering the right side can be seen distinctly in this photo. The lower part of the tumor contained a yellow pus; the top, about the size of a hazel nut, stood off wide from the body, was dark red, and covered with partially dry, wrinkled skin. The Opaline Green bird was shipped to a pathological institute and the double tumor was removed. The budgie recovered.

benefit. Be sure to wipe off dampness on the feathers after giving milk. Wet feathers will only hasten his end. Hulled or steel-cut oats will often tempt him to eat and he may soon recover. If severe bronchitis or even pneumonia has set in, there is usually not much he can do. Watery droppings usually accompany a cold. If he should develop a catarrh in the throat, he will often try to get rid of the accumulated mucus by regurgitating the seeds he has eaten.

Pullorum Disease. This well-known disease is caused by a bacillus belonging to the Salmonella group, *Salmonella pullorum.* Although many types of diarrhea are common in budgerigars, Pullorum disease has not yet been demonstrated in these birds so far as we could ascertain. Where a positive agglutination test was obtained from budgerigars, it was probably due to the *Salmonella*

Sometimes a normal molt is confused with French Molt. Compare the bird shown here to the one perched on the breeding box on page 181.

typhi murium organism (avian paratyphoid, see below), which is also pathogenic, and birds showing its presence are best destroyed. Canaries, sparrows, bullfinches, goldfinches and green finches have been found to harbor the *S. pullorum* organism, and if budgerigars are exposed to it they will indoubtedly contract it.

The mortality is most severe in young birds, but deaths among mature stock are not infrequent. It is characteristic of this disease that the pathogenic organism may be transferred from generation to generation through the eggs. It has been proved by laboratory tests that infected birds lay infected eggs and that infected chicks will hatch from these eggs. Such chicks develop very unevenly. Many are stunted in their growth, some die and some grow into mediocre birds which produce inferior young and a quantity of sterile and addled eggs. Stock infected with bacillary white diarrhea is not profitable and brings much disappointment to the owner. If adequte laboratory tests have proved the breeding troubles to be due to infection of the stock with white diarrhea, it is best to destroy the entire stock, thoroughly disinfect the breeding quarters and start over with healthy, well-producing birds. Treatment with drugs and chemicals has not always been successful; streptomycin seems most promising. Scrupulous cleanliness and the use of disinfectants will help to minimize the spread of the infection.

122

The Molt. This is not a disease, but may become one if a bird is kept in too warm a room. The temperature should not be allowed to rise above seventy-four or seventy-five degrees Fahrenheit. A bird kept in a room of eighty degrees will frequently go into a violent molt shedding feathers much too often. This will weaken his constitution, may bleach his colors, and gradually lead to ill health. A bird exposed to sunshine through glass may go into a molt from too much heat. Continuous shedding of feathers is called soft molt and must be guarded against by good care and feeding.

The largest molt in a budgerigar's life is the baby molt during which he throws off his nest feathers and grows his adult plumage. It occurs between the ages of three and five months, starting earlier or later according to the weather. The dark striations on the head extending down to the beak in the baby bird are replaced by the white or yellow feathers on the forehead of the adult bird. The small, indefinite spots around the throat (necklace) of the baby bird are dropped and replaced by three nice round spots on either side, six in all. The outer one on each side is partially covered by the elongated purplish cheek patches. The young budgie needs special attention during this time, and greens and his dose of cod-liver oil are more important than usual. Later on in life he will shed feathers sporadically, especially with changes in temperature, but he will not drop as many feathers as he does during the baby molt. The adult budgerigar has no regular season for his molt, though the summer seems to be the time when most budgies grow new feathers.

French Molt. This is not a normal molt but a feather disease peculiar to budgerigars and caused by a disturbance in metabolism. Baby budgies lose some or all of their long wing feathers and may also lose their tail feathers. According to various scientific investigations, the disease is caused by a lack of necessary foodstuffs while the birds are still in the nest. With good feeding and sensible care many of the birds so afflicted will grow normal feathers without being treated with any medicines. The use of insecticides is useless because the disease is not caused by any "bugs." None have been found and other cage birds do not develop French Molt. The disease is not catching. The more severe cases will not regrow their lost feathers and will never be

Examples of an advanced form of French Molt.

able to fly. Otherwise, the birds seem completely healthy. Such stunted feather growth, however, is undesirable and birds suffering from French Molt should not be sold. To help normal feathers to grow, a treat food from your pet shop and, of course, greens should be offered daily.

Mating Fever. A lone budgerigar may show signs of wanting to mate. Females have laid eggs on the cage floor, and males have become quite noisy and unruly. In the case of females it is best to let the little hen lay a full clutch and incubate her eggs for a while, and then remove them all at one time. In the case of males it is more difficult to stop mating fever; usually it subsides after two or three weeks. Some birds go through such a period more often than others. Change of surroundings is recommended. If a female is placed into the cage with a male, they rarely mate and the male will cease to be a good talker and pet.

The mites that cause "scaly face" can quickly be killed by two or three applications of benzyl benzoate applied with a brush.

Paratyphoid. This disease also is caused by bacteria belonging to the Salmonella group. It is found in all domestic animals and birds. Epidemics have wiped out stocks in bird stores and aviaries. Although not all birds die, the survivors often pass the disease to new arrivals. The bacteria have definitely been isolated in canaries, parrots, siskins, goldfinches and other finches. General symptoms of illness were observed. Some birds seemed to suffer from constipation at the beginning. The characteristic symptom, however, is a greenish diarrhea. Again, treatment by drugs is rarely effective.

Newcastle Disease. This disease affects all birds and some mammals, even man. The disease has been demonstrated in parrakeets, and we have to be very careful to protect our budgie aviaries from infection. The virus may be carried into the aviary from an infected poultry yard. The death rate in baby chicks may reach 100 percent.

Symptoms resemble those of bronchitis; in addition, there is serious involvement of the nerves. Twisting of the head, abnormal egg shell formation and loose droppings are common. The legs are partially or completely paralyzed, twitching of the wings and body is marked, and in fatal cases the birds are no longer able to eat and eventually die. In less severe cases they survive and recover partially but not completely. The disease, caused by a virus, is contagious.

After the diagnosis has been obtained, an attempt to vaccinate the remaining birds may be made, but success is doubtful in the case of birds as small as budgerigars.

Summer Sickness. Every pet shop and bird hospital receives many frantic calls in the summer, especially after a spell of extremely hot weather, about pet budgies having been taken ill. It seems that a variety of symptoms and causes are involved in these summer ills. One of the main complaints is a cold. For example, a bird has been exposed to cross ventilation and draft from open windows or from the air current of a fan or air-conditioning unit. He has difficulty in breathing and sits with wings opened to get air; often his eyes are closed, but his head is not tucked under the feathers. This generally means congestion of air passages and the bird should be treated as mentioned above under "Colds."

126

At other times digestive disturbances, often caused by drinking foul water, are predominating. Budgies generally do not drink much water but in hot weather they do. At such times fresh water should be given two or three times daily and the water cup should be washed daily in hot soap suds and then well rinsed. All the bird's eating dishes should be washed as carefully as our own dishes. The cage, perches, even bells and toys must be scrubbed, rinsed, and dried. Budgerigars can withstand temperatures well above one hundred degrees if the measures mentioned are adopted. The birds should not suddenly be transferred from a hot to a cold, air-conditioned room, and they should always be kept out of draft.

Digestive Disturbances. Digestive disturbances are caused by allowing the bird to eat foods that are not part of his natural diet. A baby bird, especially, should not be allowed to eat anything but his accustomed seeds, bird treat food, and greens. As he grows older, he is able to tolerate greater variety. However, he has to be watched so that he does not pick up things from the breakfast and dinner table which may prove harmful. The closer one adheres to his natural diet, the healthier a bird will be. Don't rely on his instincts as to what he can digest; a hand-raised bird imitates his master instead of birds of his kind. If a bird is seen to vomit and throw shelled seeds out of his crop, and if these have a bad smell, he should be given a pinch of Epsom salts in his drinking water and coaxed to drink it. The cause of the trouble should be investigated and avoided in the future. If the disturbance is more severe, his stool may become green and watery and the bird may lose his appetite. Again, warm milk with whiskey is beneficial and may sustain him until he can eat normally. A bird ill in this manner for a long time usually does not completely recover. These little creatures, so hardy when kept well, are not resistant to disease. Recently a scientific publication mentioned the beneficial effects of red wine on infectious diseases. Dilute the red wine by half with water and place into the drinking cup. Regular dosing with Epsom salts or other saline solution is very harmful.

Never put a bird into a freshly painted cage or one on which the paint has been allowed to dry in droplets. The budgie may chew at a drop of paint, dry on the outside but still wet on the inside, and poison himself. If a cage is painted at home, allow it to dry for four weeks. Use leadless enamel and guard against paint drops on the wires and any accumulation of paint in corners.

Diarrhea has been cured in some cases by a little penicillin given by mouth, or by the second brew of strong tea, or by a larger supply of oats, or by sprinkling poppy seeds on some soft food he might eat. Keeping the bird warm will conserve his strength and induce him to drink. If the trouble persists, a medicine as used against diarrhea in human infants may be purchased in a drug store. It should be diluted by half with water and a medicine dropperful given into the beak once a day for three days. Repeat if necessary. Push the eye dropper far enough down into the throat so not too much of the liquid will run out. A bird store or bird hospital attendant will be of help if the owner of the sick pet is reluctant to administer the treatment himself.

Throwing Up Seeds. Many an owner of a lively budgie with no sign of illness has worried when the bird regurgitated seeds from his crop while looking into a mirror or at a shiny object. These birds by nature feed their mate and their young in this manner. Their natural instincts manifest themselves when they see their reflection and they attempt to feed the bird in the mirror. The owner does not need to be alarmed in this case.

Insert the tip of an eye dropper in the side of the mouth, at the hinge of the upper and lower beak. Usually a sick bird will grasp the tip when it is offered to him this way. Allow a drop at a time to trickle down his throat.

Egg-bound. A bird in poor health or kept in breeding quarters which are too cold, or receiving improper care and feeding, may not be able to lay an egg when it becomes due. Such a bird is egg-bound and, if not treated, will die. The condition is more common in budgies than in other cage birds, but it is rarely seen in well-run aviaries.

Egg-binding may occur while the egg is descending from the ovary and its passage is obstructed by a growth or tumor, or it will occur just inside the vent. The most common cause is soft-shell eggs. Other causes are: (1) the use for breeding purposes of immature or weak birds, or of old worn-out ones; (2) too high a temperature in breeding quarters; (3) too little calcium in the grit; (4) chill; (5) disturbance during laying. The last named may be caused by mites making the bird restless and/or spastic.

It is not hard to recognize an egg-bound hen. She shows obvious distress, sits in a peculiar position on the cage floor, and sometimes gasps for breath. In other cases the bird remains on or in the nest and its distress may not be noticed, but it may later be found dead.

When the bird is taken into the hand, the egg may easily be felt just above the vent. Slight pressure from above may dislodge it. Further treatment consists of placing the bird in a hospital cage or in a warm place. Some recommend dry heat, some steam. Placing the cage above a pan of boiling water has often helped. A soft cloth should be laid on the cage floor to save the egg when it is dropped. A little olive oil brushed on the vent or carefully inserted into the opening will aid laying.

In severe cases a prolapse, a raw fleshy structure protruding from the vent, is noticed. After the egg is laid, this structure should be pushed back into the body. Often a bird does not survive; if she does, she can never (or seldom) be used for breeding again. Mild cases as a rule allow complete recovery.

If obstruction in the upper part of the oviduct prevents the egg from descending, the hen may show signs of paralysis and often dies without the breeder being able to help her. Anatomical malformations are rare.

Soft-Shell Eggs. The failure of a hen to surround the egg with a hard shell has been ascribed to two causes. Either the bird did not receive a sufficient amount of lime or calcium or she is suffer-

Cleanliness will prevent parasites from multiplying. Spraying breeding nest-boxes in aviaries will help to kill these pests.

ing from tumors or malformation of the glands which secrete the material for the egg shell. The egg may be surrounded by a skin only and may be laid in this condition. Such an egg is often dropped on the cage floor instead of into the nest, because the hen has no control over holding an egg without a shell. Soft-shell eggs frequently cause egg-binding, the muscles not being able to grasp the egg in order to expel it. If heat treatment does not help, the egg must be punctured carefully. Some eggs are surrounded by a very thin shell which soon breaks during incubation.

Prevention consists in feeding birds plenty of grit rich in calcium and an abundant amount of greens all year round. Constitutional or anatomical defects causing softshell eggs are incurable.

Sterile or Clear Eggs. There are a number of different causes for infertile eggs. The cock may be sterile or the hen may have laid too early, before fertilization took place. A very common cause is a loose perch. A perch which rotates or is unsteady will interfere with the mating act. Anatomical abnormalities in either hen or cock may cause clear eggs. Sometimes the first clutch of eggs is sterile but the second clutch is fertile. If both clutches are infertile, the pair should be separated, rested, and then given different mates. It will then become clear which bird is at fault.

If eggs in many different nests are found sterile, the fault does not lie with the individual birds, but with the feeding. This deficiency may either be a temporary one or may have caused permanent damage to the reproductive organs. Birds raised on a poor diet are worthless as breeders.

An unfortunately frequent occurrence is that all nests have fertile eggs at the beginning of the breeding season, but towards the end almost all nests show clear eggs. The fault here, in most cases, lies in the diet. The natural reserves of the breeding birds are exhausted. The seeds should immediately be given attention. Do they germinate properly? If other possible causes of clear eggs have been investigated and remedied and still, year after year, there is trouble, seeds from a different processor should be tried.

Other causes for sterility are unfavorable conditions causing ill health, such as colds, infectious diseases, overbreeding, injudicious treatment with sulfa drugs, too long hours of artificial light, wrong management, etc. Breeding conditions should be stopped for the season. In budgies it is not necessary to pluck the feathers near the vent.

The feeding of wheat germ oil is not as effective in birds as it is in mammals. When seeds are beginning to become stale, vitamin E may be diminished and a part of the seeds may be treated with wheat germ oil and allowed to stand overnight, then mixed with twice the quantity of cod-liver oil treated seeds. Wheat germ oil and cod-liver oil should not be mixed. Lack of vitamin A, protein, fatty acids, riboflavin, biotin, and the amino acid tryptophane have been found to be factors in producing sterility. Many breeders feeding an all-around good diet never add wheat germ oil and do not complain about sterility in their birds.

During incubation of a clutch of eggs, one egg is often pushed aside. This egg, in most cases, is an empty or clear one. Guesses have been made as to why the hen pushes an empty egg to the

Colony breeding consists basically of releasing a great number of pairs in a confined area, providing suitable nest-boxes, and letting nature take its course. The disadvantages of this method are obvious.

side, even if the clutch is small and she could easily cover it along with the good eggs. One suggestion is that an empty egg cools its surroundings. Eggs containing growing embryos give off some heat, while an empty egg does not.

Broken eggs. Eggs will break when the shell is too thin (see under Soft-Shell Eggs, above.) Mice and rats may invade the nests and break and eat eggs. Outdoors snakes, squirrels, etc., will eat bird eggs. Cats may frighten setting hens into leaving the nest so abruptly as to cause egg damage. Rarely do birds eat their own eggs if properly managed and fed. However, vices like eating their eggs will develop in birds receiving insufficient care. An egg dropped in a flight cage with other birds around will often be pecked at.

In the poultry yard egg-eating by the birds is well known. Mineral and protein deficiencies have been blamed. Broken eggs are said to start the habit. As a preventative it is recommended that enough lime be fed to avert the appearance of soft-shell and thin-shell eggs.

Oversized and Undersized Eggs. It happens that healthy twins can be hatched from giant eggs, but not all giant eggs contain twins; in some instances the large size is due to an extra amount of albumen. It also happens that an egg may prove too large for a hen to lay, and she may die. On the other hand, tiny eggs the size of a bean are usually infertile and often do not contain a yolk. At times, if only moderately undersized, they produce small, weak young. A hen who persists in laying undersized eggs only should be destroyed or used as a foster mother. Although the first one or two eggs of a young hen are often too small, the remainder of the clutch is generally of normal size.

Egg size normally varies with the hens. Opaline hens, as a rule, lay larger eggs than Normals. Furthermore, the size of the eggs varies with the size of the hen and with the strain.

Dead in Shell. There are many different causes of death of embryos in the egg. If embryos of our cage birds were not so small, we could examine them regularly and possibly find the reason why they could not hatch. Deformities are often present. Such impairment of normal growth may be due to dietary deficiencies in the yolk which nourishes the embryo or to hereditary factors. Certain beak deformities have been found to be inherited. The embryo may be in the wrong position within the egg. Cooling of eggs is less often the case than assumed. Normal embryos can stand much cooling before being injured.

Shifting around of eggs by young of the previous clutch is a common cause for the failure of eggs to hatch. Too much moisture in the air prevents the egg from breathing normally. An atmosphere which is too dry will dry out the egg and toughen the membrane within the shell, and the hatching chicks will not be able to pierce it. The homeland of our budgies, Australia, is a dry continent, so it is perhaps not surprising that these birds do not prosper in an atmosphere which is too humid. If the hen feels the eggs need moistening, she will damper her breast feathers on wet greens if such are supplied in her cage.

Soiled Eggs. Eggs which show caked droppings of the birds on the shell will usually hatch. It is better not to wash them, since the shell may break or the washing may remove a natural coating on the shell which prevents germs from entering the egg. At times, however, the caked droppings are so thick that the young bird inside cannot break the shell with its egg-tooth. When the eggs are so heavily coated with droppings that the pores are sealed and bacteria can enter, the young bird may die long before hatching. Gentle washing in lukewarm water may be tried, but it is better to check on care and feeding of the parents to find the cause for the sticky droppings. Nests should be quite dry. An alert breeder who spots an egg with a live chick inside trying to hatch may often successfully save the little creature's life by gently breaking the shell.

Mice and Mites. These pests can seriously interfere with a bird's health. Seeds, contaminated with the droppings of mice, may poison a bird. A mouse might get into the budgie's cage at night and eat the seeds. Whenever mice can find seeds, mousetraps baited with cheese are useless. The traps should be baited with kernels of sunflower seeds or grains of canary seed. Poison, obtainable in drug stores, may be put where the mice but not the birds will find it.

Red mites are small parasites which feed on a bird at night, making him restless and depriving him of sleep by night and causing him to scratch all day. While gray in the evening, these pests are red in the morning because they are filled with the blood of the bird. They can be detected by covering the cage with a white cloth for the night and are seen as red dots on the white background in the morning. Discard or wash the cover immediately. Red mites do not live on the bird during the day, but retreat to crevices, ends of perches, paper on the cage floor, etc., for the day. Transfer the bird by day to a clean cage, take the infested cage and immerse it in boiling water; do the same with perches and food dishes. Cages made partly of wood should have a coat of paint or varnish.

Mites cannot exist for very long on a healthy, well-kept budgerigar. Cleanliness will prevent these parasites from multiplying. A budgie with his strong beak and everlasting preening will soon dislodge such pests, but while he is able to keep himself clean he cannot very well be expected to keep the whole cage clean.

Eating of Excrements. This is occasionally observed and has worried many an owner of a valuable bird. There is nothing to worry about, however. A bird has no conception of what excrements are. His sense of smell is not very well developed; in his natural habitat he lives in trees and his excrements drop out of sight. In captivity the droppings may be found in a dried condition under his favorite perching place. He does not recognize them and may chew on them as he does on anything else. The chances are he does not eat his droppings, but just crumbles them. Remove them frequently and he will not have a chance to pick at them.

On the other hand, if the bird does not receive a good grit containing oystershell and greens are not offered him, he may be starved for calcium or other food elements and may try to obtain these from his droppings.

Scratching. Because he takes very few baths, a budgerigar does more preening than most other birds. Frequently a newly purchased baby bird may indulge in excessive scratching during the first few weeks in his new home. Keep his cage scrupulously clean to exclude the possibility of mites causing the scratching. Usually no mites or lice are present. Excessive scratching may be caused by a change of temperature, a change in the moisture content of the air, too high a temperature, or by irritation of the skin from being handled a great deal. The feeding of cod-liver oil or spraying the bird with water often stops the scratching. When a bird commences to molt, his skin will itch and he will scratch more often than usual.

Psittacosis. This disease is also called parrot fever or ornithosis. In some isolated cases parrakeets have transmitted the infection to human beings. Vital statistics show that such cases have been extremely rare. Furthermore, the disease in man is indistinguishable from common virus pneumonia and may be treated

135

with aureomycin. The virus may also be carried and transmitted by other birds. It should be emphasized, however, that the desire of some unscrupulous breeders and dealers to place large numbers of cheap parrakeets or budgerigars on the market has resulted in the overbreeding and underfeeding of these birds. As is the case with other livestock, such practices lead to lowering of resistance and may open the door to disease. Breeders of all psittacine birds should be doubly careful to keep their aviaries in a sanitary condition, not to allow any ailing bird in their breeding quarters and not to overwork their birds.

Overgrown Beak. This ailment has been observed more often among members of the parrot family than among other birds. The cause seems to be a nutritional disturbance, as lack of necessary food factors over a long period of time. Beaks and also toenails are composed of a horny substance called keratin, a protein. A little hardboiled egg (fifteen minutes) mixed with the treat food as well as consideration of the other food factors as mentioned under Feeding is recommended. Sunlight is always beneficial for general health, but sunlight which has passed through a glass window is of no great benefit to a bird because the glass filters out most of the ultra-violet rays.

Opportunity for chewing on wood should be given to every budgie. In nature they excavate tree trunks for their nests and keep their beaks trim in this manner. Budgies live to peal off the bark of leaf bearing tree branches (not of fresh pine branches—balsam will poison them).

Overgrown beaks also may develop after a period of diarrhea caused by colds or digestive disturbances. The beak must be trimmed back and with good feeding a cure may result. In severe cases the beak must be trimmed back repeatedly with nail scissors. Avoid cutting into the live part. It is best to cut from the sides, shaping the beak to its natural length and width. If cut too short, bleeding may occur. A few drops will do no harm, but if bleeding does not stop in a minute or two, the tip of the beak should be cauterized by touching a glowing cigarette lightly to it. This does not hurt the bird. If an overgrown beak is left unattended, the bird will not be able to shell seeds.

Feather Picking. The vice of chewing on their own feathers is well known among parrot-like birds kept in captivity. The cause cannot always be determined with certainty, but there are three main reasons for a bird pulling out its small body feathers.

1. The bird has become extremely nervous from being played with too much or being kept up too long at night. On the other hand, leaving a bird that is used to much attention suddenly alone for long periods has also precipitated the trouble.
2. Stale seeds and faulty feeding.
3. A painful ingrown feather. This should be searched for with a magnifying glass and removed with tweezers.

Bare and sore spots should be covered with petroleum jelly and the bird should receive the best of care and a change of surroundings. Feather plucking should not be confused with the normal molt when a bird naturally removes loose feathers. Molting does not produce bare spots in budgerigars.

This young budgie doesn't have all its feathers, and his feet are badly spread due to lack of vitamin D.

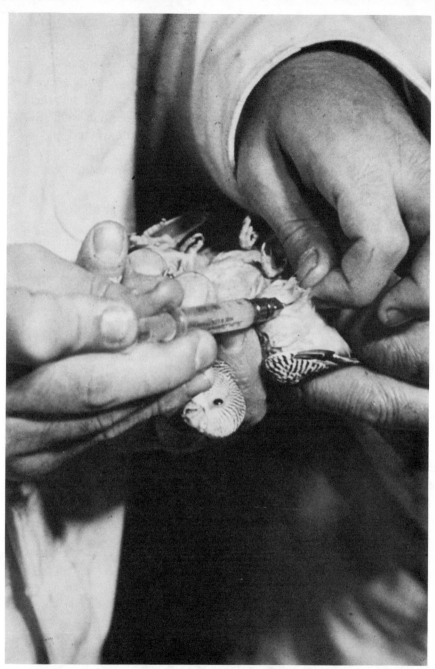

Vaccines properly used by the veterinarian or under direct veterinary medical supervision are an effective and useful part of "fencing out" disease by making animals resistant to exposure to it.

The cere of the budgie has a bright blue color in the adult male. In females, even in the nest, it is less prominent.

Discolored Cere. The cere (the waxy skin above the beak) has, as we have learned, a bright blue color in the adult male. At times a brown crust develops over the cere which makes the little cock look like a hen. This does not mean that a change in sex has taken place but it seems due to a secretion from the nostrils resulting from a cold or disturbed health. In some cases it may be due to a fungus growth. A veterinarian is able to determine whether this is so and he will prescribe for treatment.

At times small parasites, a species of mite, attack the cere and cause a whitish discoloration or honey-combed appearance on the lower part of the cere. Occasionally the beak, too, looks rough. A careful application with a mite-killing solution from your pet shop, repeated several times if necessary, will stop the trouble. Perches, cage, and surroundings should be sprayed. Great cleanliness is necessary.

Growths. Birds occasionally develop a growth or tumor. The cause is unknown. If under the skin and if not too close to the crop, such growths can be removed by a veterinarian. If internal, there is not much that can be done.

A healthy, happy bird makes a sight that won't easily be forgotten.

VIII Accidents

A budgie enjoys freedom; he does not like to be confined to his cage for any length of time. However, in order to avoid accidents, it sometimes is safer to lock him up when he has to be left alone. The kind of room in which he is kept may determine whether or not he may safely be left out all day without supervision. It may be helpful to mention some of the causes of accidents: one bird, kept in the dining room, fell into a pitcher half full of water. If the owner had not been near, the budgie would have surely drowned as there was no way for him to escape unaided. Another hung himself in a cord from a window shade with which he had been playing, but he too was rescued in time. Another was found wedged between a half open window and screen. One started flying in the dark and fell behind a bookcase. One broke his leg in the pulley of a clothesline in the kitchen.

Other accidents: one bird was stepped on. Being so very tame, he was too trusting to get out of the way of the approaching foot. One was caught in a swing door and one in an ordinary door, both while trying to follow their master. One, kept in a round cage, forced his head through a space where the wires were too far apart, then worked up where the wires were closer together. He was strangled before help arrived. One, which was kept locked up too much in a small cage, performed so many contortions that he dislocated a joint in his leg. One, still a baby with wing-feathers insufficiently clipped, went in full flight against an uncovered window and broke his neck.

The most frequent cause of losing a tame budgie is letting him escape into the open. The bird is so bewildered by the strangeness of a sky and unlimited space instead of a ceiling and walls that he flies and flies until out of sight. If advertised for, a bird might be returned by an honest finder, but only too often the pet remains lost.

If the bird can be seen in the branches of a near-by bush or tree, he may be coaxed back by showing him his cage or favorite mirror. If this does not work, a shower with the garden hose may be effective since it has brought back many budgies. His feathers become so wet that he cannot fly and is therefore easily picked up. If the bird is seen high up in a tree at night, the owner will have to get up before sunrise the next morning before the bird wakes up and begins to travel to remote places. Again the above attempts at catching him may be used. Budgies frequently join a group of sparrows. They have been seen eating with them and roosting with them at night. A budgie who has been taught to recite his home address and/or telephone number has frequently been returned by an honest finder.

Where a bird is kept in a country cottage for the summer, it may be advisable to keep his wing feathers clipped so that if he does escape through a screen door he can easily be recaptured. One bird rode out on the back of a dog and when the dog was called, the bird returned with him. Luckily he stayed with his mount.

In a number of cases a bird alighted on the shoulder of his master and the latter, unaware of the presence of the bird on his shoulder, walked out of the house. It is advisable to always spot a bird before going out. Only when the little budgie is seen on his playground or in one of his favorite places is it safe to leave the house.

Christmas tree branches and ornaments have poisoned budgies who chewed on them. Their desire to chew should be satisfied by supplying a piece of soft wood nailed to the playstand. Better still, branches of fruit trees or other leaf-bearing trees should be provided if they are free of insect spray. Budgies love to peel off the bark of branches. Female budgies, especially, have a strong desire to chew and this urge should be satisfied. No balsam, pine or cedar branches should be used. Be sure that the branches have not been sprayed with insecticides. If uncertain, better wash them under a strong spray of hot water.

To guard against accidents a tame budgie must at times be locked in his cage. It is often difficult to do this since the bird does not want to be locked up and will do everything possible to prevent it. Some owners have pulled down the shades. In a darkened room the budgie assumes it is time to go to bed and will retire to his cage. Placing greens, oats, or toys in his cage or touching his bells in the cage may bring a budgie home. Walking into a closet with the bird on the shoulder, then closing the door and, in the dark,

Too many birds in a much too small aviary. It is almost impossible to avoid accidents in such housing!

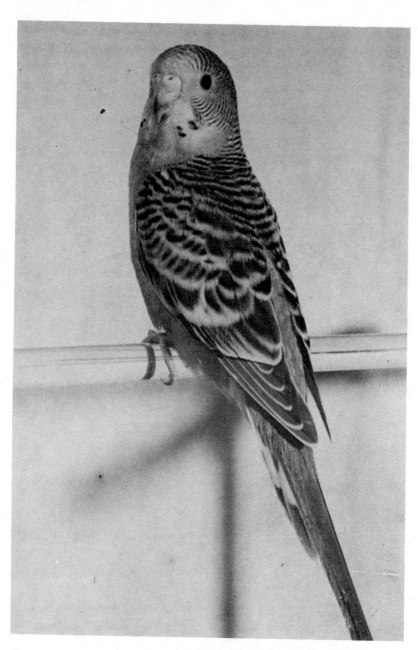

A young cock of excellent substance and quality. Regardless of the quality of a pet budgie, its owner is under obligation to provide it with an environment free of health hazards and accident causers.

A playground affords a means of keeping a budgie happily occupied. So does this barnyard. Because they often get rough treatment from a playful budgie, toys must be made of wood or hard plastic. Our personal preference is for the plastic, which is easier to clean and less likely to be chewed, and therefore is less dangerous to their health. The barn shown here is much too small and therefore unsuitable.

gently closing a hand over him will work until the budgie learns about this trick.

Never try to catch your bird by pressing a thumb on his foot when he is sitting on the hand. He will never want to perch on a hand again. Be sure no loose ends of wires or loops of string are anywhere about. It has happened that a budgie caught his leg band in one and got entangled in the other.

This account of disasters might give the impression that a little budgie cannot last very long. However, most of these little creatures delight their owners for many years and even outlive them. The majority never have their cage door closed and have the run of the house without mishap. But the occasional loss of a talking budgerigar has caused such severe heartaches that the danger of accidents cannot be overstressed.

An inexpensive indoor flight which one can walk into.

All perches should be set firmly in place, care being exercised to see that they are not set one below another in such a way as to have the birds below soiled by the droppings from the birds above. Avoid swinging perches.

Budgie with typical Pied markings. If one likes a beautiful talker or pet, a Pied bird is just it! Watch, however, the color in Pieds closely—there is strong tendency for these birds to show only small areas of dark coloring and consequently lose much of their charms.

Budgerigars will breed better if several nest-boxes (8½ in. high, 6 in. square, with a round opening approximately 1½ in. in diameter) are kept near each other where the friendly birds can see their neighbors.

IX History
of the Budgerigar

The first description of the budgerigar comes to us from Shaw at the turn of the 18th century in "Naturalist's Miscellany" (1789-1813) and in "Zoology of Holland." The first bird of this species was shown in the Museum of the Linnaean Society in London in 1831 and was described as a rare specimen. Then the famous English natural scientist John Gould gave us a most interesting account of the life of this small parrot in "The Birds of Australia" (1848). In seven magnificent volumes, beautifully illustrated and dedicated to Queen Victoria, Gould described all Australian birds, among them our budgerigar (*Melopsittacus undulatus*). Other names of the budgerigar are: Warbling Grass Parrakeet, Undulated Parrakeet, Canary Parrot (so named by the colonists on account of its constant warbling), Betcherrygar (meaning "pretty bird" in the dialect of the natives of the Liverpool plains). The word budgerigar, now commonly used, was derived from betcherrygar.

It was John Gould who brought the first living budgerigar to Europe in 1840. From then·on these hardy little birds were imported in increasing numbers. As Hans Steiner (in a study published in Zurich, Switzerland) pointed out, there developed during this period a steadily growing interest in keeping birds and other animals in captivity. Zoological gardens were founded and books on ornithology and aviculture were published. At the end of the 19th century, 600,000 pairs of living birds were imported to France. Most of the shipments of budgerigars went to England, and breeders in the Netherlands soon distinguished themselves by raising these birds. The first large aviary for this purpose was built in the Zoological Garden of Antwerp around 1870 although small establishments had already raised them since 1850. With the increasing demand, more aviaries sprang up on the continent and in England, and also more birds were imported from Australia. Finally the imports grew to such an extent that it no longer paid to

149

This lithograph, taken from *Naturalist's Miscellany,* published in London around 1800, is the earliest depiction of a parrakeet on record. It was drawn by Dr. Lear and lithographed by Nodder.

The lone chick, favored by some extremists in the quest for grand prize winners.

breed budgerigars commercially. Then, in 1894, an embargo was put on budgerigars in Australia and the imports suddenly stopped. Aviaries in the south of France, where the climate is as favorable as in California for breeding on a large scale, developed to the size of around 100,000 birds in one establishment. Smaller aviaries operated all over Europe and soon the first new colors of this bird made their appearance.

Color Varieties

The body color of the original budgerigar imported from Australia is light green with a yellow mask and black and yellowish shell-like markings on the wings. All other colors now seen in captivity have sprung from this original green bird. The first to appear was the yellow bird with a faint green suffusion on the breast and rump. It first appeared in Belgium in 1872. Soon more birds of this color were bred in other European countries. In Belgium there also appeared the first blue budgerigar, in 1878, but this variety disappeared again until 1910. The blue budgerigar is a green budgerigar with the yellow pigment missing. The faint green suffusion of the yellow budgerigar indicates, however, that not all the blue pigment is missing. A trace remains, giving us the faint green. The white variety first appeared in 1917. This bird is not entirely white, but has a faint blue suffusion on the breast and rump and, like the yellow bird, has faint gray wing markings.

Fabulous prices were paid for the new colors as long as they were still scarce. W. Watmough reports that one hundred to two hundred pounds were paid in England for one pair. A.W. Wilson tells us that a Japanese prince, in 1925, was so intrigued by the beautiful blue color of some budgerigars he saw in England that he purchased one pair and took it home to Japan to give it to his bride-to-be as a love token. From then on a vogue developed in Japan to give a pair of lovebirds to one's beloved. English breeders were not able to fill all the orders received from Japan, and in 1927 prices for one pair of blue lovebirds (budgerigars) went up to 1,000 dollars. However, a short time later prices fell again. The Japanese, being experienced in raising all kinds of birds, started to raise blue lovebirds themselves; furthermore the importation of these birds was stopped by the Japanese government. Thus ended the most prosperous period for English breeders, but the name lovebird still clings to the little budgerigar.

In 1919 the olive green variety was first reported and in 1921 mauve and cobalt budgerigars made their appearance. Since then the beautiful graywing varieties appeared in all colors. The new cinnamons are most pleasing birds. They are available in green, mauve, blue, yellow, and white. Their body colors are lighter than in the normal varieties and their wing markings show a cinnamon color in place of the black markings. Their feathers have a silky sheen and delicate texture. They should not be confused with the more common graywing varieties. Cinnamon budgerigars show a brown color on the midrib of the long tail and wing feathers, while graywings show a gray color.

Opaline budgerigars are becoming very popular; they are gorgeous birds and make exceedingly good talkers. The blue or

A young Lutino, which is the albinistic phase in the Green series. Richness of color is very desirable, along with complete lack of any green suffusion. This color variety is sex-linked. The depth of rich yellow combined with the albinistic red eye makes this an attractive variety that has found great favor with the fancy.

The hope and dream of all budgerigar breeders is to be able to produce champions and one day to have their budgies surrounded by winning ribbons.

Opposite:
This Sky Blue budgie is far from being a good example of the type of bird which wins the show! It is out of all proportion and fails very badly to conform to the "ideal budgerigar." The bird carries far too much fat on the chest, has a very heavy stomach and carries too much under the perch and behind the perch; in addition the tail of the bird drops—the whole contour of the bird is nothing like that of the ideal budgie.

155

green breast color extends over the back and through the wings and the back of the head is white or yellow. Golden Cobalts and Yellow-faced Blues are equally beautiful. In some specimens there is a faint yellow film extending over the blue which gives such birds a luminous appearance. Progressive budgerigar breeders have produced blue Opalines with yellow faces and white wings; some of these are "Rainbows."

Among the pink-eyed varieties are the pure yellow ones called Lutinos and the pure white ones called Albinos. There are black-eyed Lutinos and pure white budgies with black eyes. Fallows, on the other hand, carry pigmentation in their feathers but have pink eyes. Some Fallows are pure white. There are Brownwings, Clear-wings, White and Yellowflighted, and Harlequins. These gorgeous new colors can be seen at local and national bird shows.

Violet budgerigars are of a deep cobalt shade and still rare. Additional shades are in existence but are as yet practically unobtainable. However, the desire of the pet-loving public to have in their homes not only a budgie of exceptional talking ability but also of exceptional coloring is increasing at such a rate that it will not be long before our foremost budgerigar breeders will be able to supply the fancier with the rare shades of budgerigars.

The Budgerigar in the United States

What the large aviaries in southern France did for budgerigar breeding has been repeated in this country in California where the climate is favorable for outdoor breeding. The first breeding experiments in this state were undertaken by J.C. Edwards in 1910. The first large aviary was built in 1924; others followed until a three million dollar a year industry developed. The industry has suffered various reverses since then, the parrot fever scare destroying much of it and causing the rare shades to disappear. At the present time aviaries are springing up all over the country. Our southern states are producing budgerigars in great numbers. At the same time it becomes apparent that the climate in the north does not interfere with the raising of fine birds.

Yellow Wing light Green cock. Pet-trade type!

An almost perfectly marked White Flighted Pied Opaline... as far as the right wing is concerned. (Another major fault is the lack of pure white tail feathers.)

History of the Talking Budgerigar

The first reports of a talking budgerigar came to us from Germany. There, as early as 1877, a young budgerigar kept without a mate imitated the melodies of a song bird, later the call of a pair of zebra finches and then, kept away from all other birds, the voice of his master. This bird learned several little phrases. Since then accounts of birds which learned a number of words have become more frequent in Europe. Today the talking budgerigar is well known in England. The first report of an American talking budgie came from California in 1930. This bird was nine months old and could say twenty words. Since then the fame of these amazing

Head study of a great Green cock. Note the width of skull, depth of bib and size of spots.

birds has rapidly spread in this country and the number of pets kept in homes is constantly on the increase. Canada can boast of a number of talking budgies. From the south there have come reports of Spanish-speaking budgies. But to many Americans the talents of this little bird are still unknown. Some people still believe that budgerigars can be kept only in pairs and will die if kept singly. Even if it is explained that hand-raised birds are different, that they are trained to be alone and do not know anything else but human companionship, many people remain skeptical.

Two well bred young Lutinos, the red-eyed, albinistic phase of the green series.

X Other Parakeets And Parrots

The history of the talking parakeet* (not budgerigar) goes back to the days of Alexander the Great. Under his reign (336-323 B.C.) beautiful parakeets were imported from India and its islands. Some were subsequently called Alexandrine Parrots, others Ringnecked Parakeets. They acquired great popularity as pets. Many of Alexander's generals owned specimens which were outstanding talkers. They are about the size of a small pigeon.

Aristotle, who lived at the same time as Alexander the Great, also mentions these parakeets in his writings. He describes the wonderful ability of these birds to imitate and their faithful articulation of human speech. Ovid's favorite pet was a parakeet. When it passed on, Ovid composed a long and beautiful elegy in praise of this bird. At the time of Nero, the Greeks and Romans are known to have kept Alexandrine and Ringnecked Parakeets. These birds were called "human-tongued." Nero employed explorers who, according to Pliny, ventured into Africa and obtained parrots which they brought back to Rome for eating and for pets.

Columbus brought the first American parrots to Europe. During the ensuing era of exploring, seamen returned with parrots from all over the world. Among them the Alexandrine and the Ringnecked Parakeet were imported again after they had not been seen in Europe for many, many years.

Monks in their secluded monasteries trained many birds of the parrot family. In 1550 Cardinal Ascanius bought a talking Alexandrine Parakeet for a hundred gold crowns. This bird could say clearly and without mistakes the Twelve Articles of Faith. Beautiful cages were built for these precious birds. Some were made of carved ivory and wood inlaid with mother of pearl. Others were made of ebony decorated with silver, others of tortoise shell.

* To differentiate readily between the members of the parakeet family, the editors spell the name of the family and the larger members of it with a single r. Only the names of the Grass and Shell groups (the small-sized birds) are spelled with a double r.

The Galah, or Rose Breasted Cockatoo *(Eolophus r. roseicapillus)*, is the most abundant, lowest priced and best breeder of the Cockatoo family. It is another of nature's beautiful creations and is further proof that Australia is the habitat of some of the most wonderful birds in the world.

Major Mitchell's Cockatoo *(Cacatua leadbeateri leadbeateri)* is an ideal aviary bird and a good breeder, and it occasionally makes a good household pet. The objection to Leadbeater's Cockatoo (as this bird is also known) is its rackety voice, which in reality is not as loud as that of several other Cockatoos.

At the present time, the large Yellow Head and African Gray are considered the best talkers among the large parrots. Some of the most famous birds of these species have learned to say fifty to sixty

This is "Sailor," the African Gray Parrot who sings rude songs and dances his own version of the hornpipe.

sentences and long poems and nursery rhymes. Their power of associating words with actions is quite remarkable. However, the screech of some of the Ringnecked and Alexandrine Parakeets is so bad that the shrill voice of the Amazons is considered trifling in comparison. If one of the large parrots is aroused to anger, he may prove a formidable enemy. One Great Salmon-crested Cockatoo has kept seven men armed with spades and long brooms in a corner. Some parrots have cut down to the bone when biting into a finger.

The budgerigar is not noisy; he cannot bite like a parrot. His talking voice is smaller, but more distinct. The best-bred and best-

164

Finsch's Conures are attractive red and green conures, with red on the head almost restricted to the forehead. Finsch's Conure is smaller than the Cherry Headed or Wagler's Conure.

trained specimens are superior to other talking birds as far as clarity of talking voice is concerned. They learn to associate words with incidents. They will learn to recite correctly poems and nursery rhymes thirty-five and more words long. In short, they do make ideal pets. They are now taking the place of large parrots and even of dogs in city apartments.

The Red-collared Lorikeet *(Trichoglossus haematodus rubritorquis)* is one of the most readily available members of the Lory family. It is the best breeder of all Lories in captivity and, in the wild state, is found in Australia.

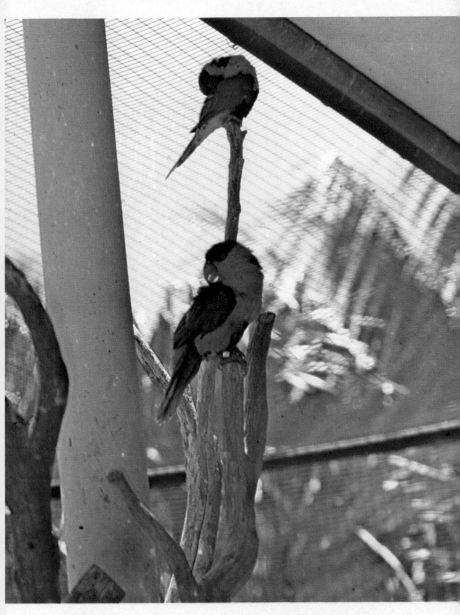

The Black-capped Lory *(Lorius lory lory)* from New Guinea. Members of the genus *Lorius* are taken to be the most typical of the large family of Lories and Lorikeets. All members of the family are very beautiful; they are rare in captivity but are ideal aviary birds if they can be obtained.

The Blue-winged Parrotlet *(Forpus passerinus vividus),* is a small bright green bird and a miniature of the African Love Bird in every respect except the bill, which is smaller.

XI Breeding

If the owner of a pet budgie decides to obtain a mate for his bird and tries to raise a family of budgies, it is not necessary to buy expensive equipment. Budgies have bred in any kind of cage and have laid eggs in various types of cavities, such as a gourd, or the partially opened drawer of a dresser, or a partially covered basket. The best and most sanitary way of breeding budgies, however, is to confine each pair to a breeding cage with a nest box attached. It is best to acquire two to three pairs, since budgies breed better when they can see other pairs of their kind. As mentioned above, pet budgies often do not breed satisfactorily. It is advisable, therefore, to obtain, good, untamed breeding stock.

For breeding the birds should be one year old, in good health and good feather, and not molting. They should be housed where they are not disturbed too much and not exposed to drafts. Lights should not keep them awake long after sundown. Where they cannot be kept in a room by themselves, the fronts of the cages should be covered with a dark cloth at night.

Correct feeding is important for the successful raising of young (see chapter on Feeding). Plenty of oyster shell should always be in the grit and a good nestling food should be fed. The parent birds may not care for the unaccustomed food at first, but with young in the nest they usually begin to eat it.

The breeding season in this country generally is from fall through spring. Except for northern regions, the summers are too hot for breeding. Sometimes individual pairs are slow to start breeding, but if healthy they will eventually begin to lay. The eggs are white and one is laid every other day. The hen incubates from the first day on. After 18 days the first chick hatches, followed by the others on alternate days. Usually not all eggs hatch. Not more than four or at the most five young should be allowed in one nest. Budgerigars are loving and devoted parents and feed their young at regular intervals.

Before the young of the first clutch are independent, the hen begins to lay her second clutch of eggs. When the young are about

The sire of these nestlings was a Gray Green Longflight, split to Blue
and carrying the sex-linked Lutino factor in a recessive state. The
female was a Cobalt budgie. Result: one Lutino (this has to be a hen),
one Sky Normal (sex not yet determined) and a Dark Gray Green
Longflight male chick split to Blue. Either of the Normal chicks, if
cocks, could be split to the Ino factor; the Blue obviously would be
split to Albino. (If you are interested in color-breeding budgerigars,
read *Breeding Budgerigars* by the same authors of this book and
published by TFH Publications, Neptune, N.J.)

The ideal budgerigar. On the continent of Europe, budgerigars are judged on the point system, while in the British Isles and America judging is done by comparison only.

six weeks old, they should be removed and given flight space for exercise and best development. After two nests of young have been raised, the nest box must be taken down to stop further breeding. Any eggs of the third clutch which may be found in the nest box should be destroyed and the parent birds given flight space for a rest period of about six months.

If the owner wants to train the young to be tame pets, it is of great help to handle the babies in the nest for a while whenever the nest box is cleaned. This saves much time later on. Such early training is usually started when the young are three weeks old.

Egg-binding occurs when the hen is unable to pass the egg. She sits in a corner of the cage or moves about with obvious distress. Placing her in a very warm spot, either in a hospital cage set at about 90 degrees or in a small cage above a kettle of boiling water (watch that she does not get too hot) usually brings about the laying of the egg. It helps to insert a bit of mineral or olive oil into the vent. A hen may become egg bound from chill·when the room temperature has dropped below forty-five degrees, the grit lacks calcium, or the food is not what is should be. (See under Health and Disease.)

Mites (see chapter on Health and Disease) should be kept from infesting nest boxes by spraying a mite-killing solution under the double nest box bottoms with a hand-spray. This is done about every other day when the concave bottom is replaced by a clean one after all young have hatched. A nest with eggs in it should not be disturbed. When all young have hatched a tablespoonful of cedar shavings is placed in the nest box each time it is cleaned.

Feather plucking of the young by the mother is often due to overbreeding or underfeeding or both. Any disturbance in nutrition such as diarrhea from faulty care and feeding or an unsuitable grit mixture, possibly also an excess of certain minerals in the diet, may cause the trouble. Either the young should be transferred to another nest containing young of similar size, or the mother should be removed. The father will in most cases raise the young alone.

This is a sturdy, very heavy bird as one would expect from a lone chick. But the lone chick is going out of favor among the big exhibitors, who feel that some of the giants are getting coarse!

Two steps in the ringing of a chick:
Left: the front two toes are being pushed through the closed band, the first step in banding.

Below: three toes have already been placed through the band. Banding is not a difficult chore if care is taken and the banding is done at the right time.

Wet nests are caused by diarrhea of the young. The feeding should be checked. If too many greens are fed at one time or the nestling food is moist instead of fairly dry and crumbly or the parents have colds, trouble will ensue. Excrement sticking to the feet or food adhering to the beak must be peeled off.

Closed numbered leg bands to be placed on the bird's foot when about one week to ten days old can be obtained from one of the budgerigar societies. The society keeps a record of these bands, which may be purchased by members.

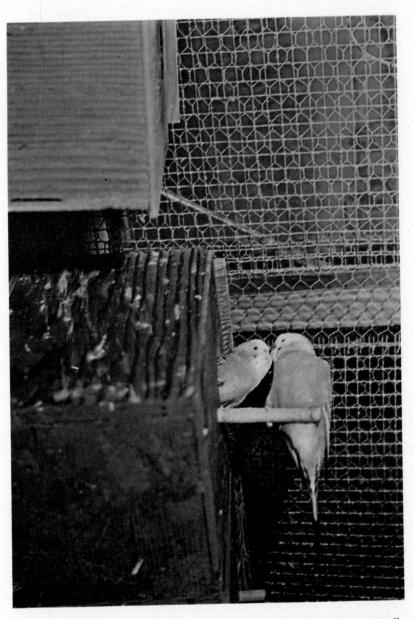

When budgerigars are well fed and housed under sanitary conditions, they suffer very few ailments.

The scope of this book does not permit a treatise on breeding. There are detailed books* on every phase of budgerigar keeping and breeding obtainable from the publisher of this book. A national magazine featuring regular articles on budgerigars is *American Cage-Bird Magazine,* 3449 N. Western Avenue, Chicago, Illinois. The national budgerigar societies, as well as some of the local budgerigar societies, give information in their monthly club bulletins.

Mention should be made of "Halfsiders." These bi-colored birds show green on one side and blue on the other, or cobalt on one side and white on the other, etc. They are very rare.

Some breeders specialize in purebred colors; some in only one or two colors; some in size, type, or new shades. Those specializing in breeding talkers will select the relatives of the best talkers for breeding. As mentioned in Chapter five, there are differences in the voices of the various talkers. After a while a good talking strain will be established.

Whether a tame and talking budgie can be used for breeding depends on how the bird was kept. If he has frequently seen birds of his kind he may make a good breeder. If he previously has learned to say a few phrases while seeing and hearing other birds, he may retain his vocabulary while breeding. Such birds are usually mediocre talkers and delight in much bird talk mixed with "human talk," but are just as much loved by their owners who may never have heard one of the exceptionally good talkers. Good talkers develop only with diligent training and when they establish close relationships with their human companions, but rarely breed successfully. In fact they will be unhappy with other birds. Many examples are on record showing that such birds will not mate or that they cause bloody fights in the nest box, driving their mates to despair. As a result of such an experience they usually lose some of their attachment to their owners and their talking suffers greatly in quality.

---

* See: *Breeding Budgerigars* by Cessa Feyerabend and Dr. Matthew M. Vriends (T.F.H. Publications, Inc., Neptune, 1978).

XII Bird Shows

Local and national exhibitions of cage birds are becoming more popular every year. In some bird shows, classes for talking birds and for trick birds are added to the many classes for untamed birds which are exhibited for their color and their elegant appearance.

Pet budgies have been exhibited with their playstand enclosed in glass or transparent plastic. To the delight of many spectators the bird tosses his toys about most of the day and climbs ladders and does his amazing tricks. Blue ribbons or a trophy or big silk rosette can be earned by such a display.

In order to be entered in a class for talking birds, a budgerigar has to be a very good talker. He should be one of those not too plentiful specimens who has been trained alone, out of sight and hearing of other budgies. He should not have any bird talk, or hardly any, in his vocabulary. All his uttered sounds should be words. Such a bird usually is stimulated to make a noise himself when he hears the many bird voices about him in the exhibition hall. He then will talk a great deal, while a mediocre talker in strange surroundings usually does not talk at all but utters bird talk only.

A candidate for a prize in a class for talking birds is usually exhibited in his own cage while the other birds are placed in standard show cages.

Washing a bird. Outward appearance is important. A budgie to be exhibited should be neat and clean looking. The pastel colors may need a bath before the great event. At times it is only necessary to wash the wing tips or the face, at other times the whole bird needs to be soaped. This should be done not less than one week before the show.

The hand bowl in the bathroom with running hot and cold water is the most convenient place. Every budgie, even if tame, bites when being washed. Therefore it is best to wrap the bird in a towel which may be shifted while washing different parts.

A man's shaving brush is soft and will not fray the feathers. Lukewarm soap suds should be used. Many prefer to use a

Each year brings larger entries and greater interest in shows as more earnest breeders and enthusiasts realize the vast potential of the exhibition budgerigar.

detergent instead of soap; it does not leave a scum on the feathers. First one wing then the other is spread out on the rim of the bowl, soaped from both sides and then rinsed with a shaving brush full of clear, warm water. The water in the bowl must be changed frequently. When all soap has been removed from the feathers, the bird is wrapped in a warm, clean towel and after much of the moisture has been absorbed by the towel, he is placed in a warm hospital or other cage. It is most important that all drafts be excluded. The cage has to be very clean.

Birds which do not need to be soaped are sprayed with cool water three or four times at about two day intervals. The bird is allowed to become wet during the last three days. During this time he preens and the natural oil gives his coat of feathers a beautiful luster.

Insurance. Some owners of a valuable budgie in an expensive cage may worry about having their precious pet in the exhibition hall for several days and nights. However, guards are supplied by the show committee and in addition a bird may be insured against theft.

178

A pair of hen budgerigars exhibited at a German show. They exhibit deep color and are in good condition. They are rather nice hens but could use greater depth in bib and smaller, more tucked-in beaks.

Proudly perched in the cage decorated by the rosettes it has won, this Green budgerigar had made his owner and breeder proud and happy.

The bird perched upon the nest box is sick, being afflicted with French Molt. French Molt is a disease in which the flight and tail feathers of very young birds break off or fall out.

Budgerigar affected with "scaly face" disease, familiar to poultrymen and fanciers. This condition (properly called cnemidocoptic pilae) is caused by a mite.

This hybrid macaw (Scarlet Macaw x Blue and Gold Macaw) shows characteristics of both of its parent species. The vivid sunset colors on the underparts are brighter and more attractive than on most hybrids between the Scarlet and the Blue and Gold. The age of this bird in this photograph is 98 days and the weight 869 grams—which is considerably less than the bird weighed when photographed at 73 days of age.

Opposite:
The Black-masked Lovebird (*Agapornis personata)* is very popular and easily bred.

XIII Purchasing a Pet Budgerigar

Several points must be kept in mind when purchasing a baby budgerigar to be trained as a pet and talker. First of all, select a bird store or aviary in which the budgerigars are kept in sanitary quarters and where all birds are healthy and alert-looking. Do not buy a bird from a store where you see sickly birds sitting in corners or where some birds are crippled. Deformed beaks, legs, or feet mean poor stock. Some breeders prefer quantity to quality and overbreed their birds, thus causing rickety young which are small in size and are an easy prey to disease. The budgerigar societies recommend that no more than two nests be taken from a pair of budgies in a year and not more than four young be raised in each nest. Naturally the price of young raised in this manner is higher than that of young from breeders who allow their birds to raise nest after nest, often with eight or ten young to a nest. Such birds are undernourished and not strong enough to eat a sufficient amount of food to sustain themselves at the time they should be sold and tuition for talking should begin. They may carry disease germs or pick up infections easily.

In Chapter one, the owners of Mickey, Socrates, Blue Boy, and Mucki related that they received their birds at the age of six weeks. Such birds had previously been tamed. There are no feeding problems with birds of that age, for the breeder has taken care of all that. If you cannot find a breeder experienced in raising potential talkers, you might take your chance with a five-week-old bird, provided that the seller can assure you that the young budgie has been out of the nest for several days and has learned to feed himself. Only well-bred birds from small nests will be independent eaters at that time. A poorly bred bird may die unless hand-fed. Hand-feeding is difficult for a person not experienced with the procedure. Also, young five-week-old budgies do not easily take to hand-feeding, for they are already too old for that.

A Green cock. There is not much wrong with this beautiful bird!

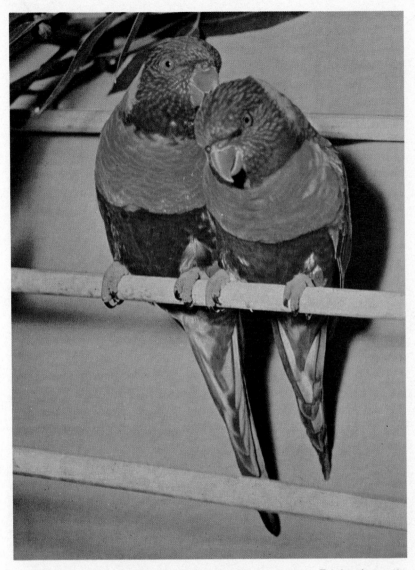

Adult Swainson's Blue Mountain Lorikeets (genus *Trichoglossus*). This is one of the most beautiful and entertaining of all the members of the parrot family.

The White Cockatoo (*Cacatua alba*), from Indonesia, is a rare bird in aviculture. It is known for its loud screech.

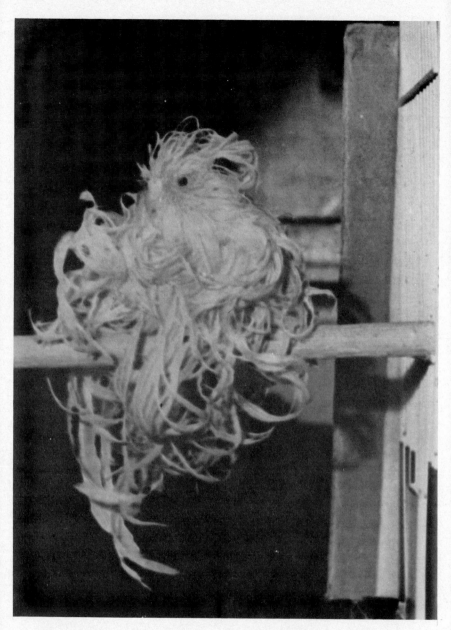

"If you put him on the end of a stick you would have a good feather duster!" A strange mutation once on display at the Essendon Society's Annual Show in the Kensington City Hall, March, 1960. It is just a matter of taste...

If possible, obtain a young male budgerigar. Although more and more reports of talking females have been received, the males as a rule make better talkers.

It is very hard to tell the sex of the young at the time when they have to be sold for potential talkers. At the age of six months it is easy to tell the males from the females, for then the male birds have a blue cere (the waxy skin around the nostrils) while the females have a tan or brown cere. Baby birds, however, show an indefinite fleshy color on their cere in both sexes. In the males it is uniformly pinkish or purplish, while in the females there is a white rim around each nostril and the edges of the cere are sometimes bluish. After the age of seven or eight weeks the cere in both sexes looks somewhat alike until the blue or tan of the adult bird develops. Some breeders can make a pretty good guess at the sex of at least some of the baby birds. They know that the females bite harder when first handled. Some females, with a little extra effort in tutoring, develop into good talkers. They easily learn to whistle melodies. They are more gentle and do not roam about the house as much as a male.

Life is hard indeed for fanciers who specialize in raising budgerigars for potential talkers. In the first place, they must keep only the best of stock. It takes much time and patience to teach a young budgie to talk and when he finally does, he will be greatly admired. Therefore, he should, of course, be a well-marked bird, rich and even in color, not patchy on the breast unless molting. He should not have faults, such as deformities, a hunched back, permanently missing wing feathers, missing toes, or bad carriage. He should stand up proudly on his perch. It is of special importance that the bird does not suffer from chronic diarrhea. Before purchasing a young budgie the vent should be examined. Do not buy a bird whose feathers around the vent are stained; this may be a sign of illness. Young birds when handled more than they are used to often develop a temporary form of loose droppings from nervousness which will soon pass. This does not stain the vent feathers.

The fancier who raises first-rate birds has to pay high prices for his breeding stock. Also such birds are expensive to keep because they can only be allowed to produce eight young a year per pair. The young have to be taken out of the nest and handled several

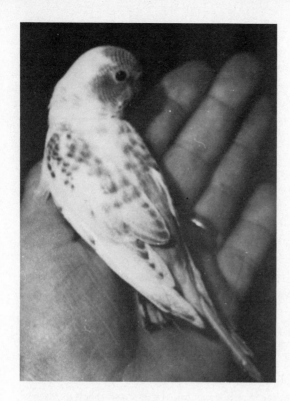

Distinguishing between a mature bird and a young budgie is easy. Note the striped forehead on this immature Pied bird. A mature budgie loses these stripes.

times each day in order to make them tame and unafraid of the human hand. When they are ready for sale they have to be sold within a few days or they may not learn to talk. The buyer of a potential talker should realize all these difficulties and should be prepared to pay a price commensurate with the painstaking way in which the young budgerigar has been raised.

After a bird of good quality has been taught to talk, he is worth as much as a talking parrot and can always be sold for a good price. The price depends on what the bird can say, whether his vocabulary is of general interest, whether he talks clearly, whether he can also whistle a melody, how tame and affectionate he is, and how old he is. A budgerigar wearing a closed leg band with the initials of a society stamped on it gives the buyer an assurance that this bird was bred by a member of the fancy who subscribes to the leading publications in the field and keeps abreast of latest developments in breeding and feeding budgerigars properly. The American Budgerigar Society and others on the east and west coast are large national organizations. Local budgerigar societies are formed in various states and members attend monthly meetings and discussion groups.

A closed leg band bears the code number or letter assigned to the breeder, the number of the bird, the year in which the bird hatched, and the initials of the society. This enables the buyer of a talking budgerigar to tell the age of the bird. Such a leg band is slipped over the foot of a baby bird when he is only a few days old. The band cannot be removed later. A budgerigar may live from fifteen to twenty years and if he should change hands several times, this record on the leg band is very valuable. However, a talking budgie is rarely offered for sale on the open market. People become so attached to such a bird that they would not think of parting with it unless forced to do so. It should be mentioned in this connection that a talking budgerigar will become attached to a new owner within a short time. However, he will be homesick for a few days, usually eating nothing during the first day and very little for several days. After that he will feel at home and eat well. It is advisable to leave the newly acquired talker confined to his cage most of the time during the first days of adjustment so that he will become acquainted with his cage and be near his food.

There are a few trainers who do not need budgerigars but buy a baby bird from a reliable source, teach it to talk and then sell it without difficulty.

Stock birds in an exhibitors' aviary.

INDEX